THE
COST OF THE
KINGDOM

When asked to write a commendation for this book, I groaned – another task with a dead-line – but then I started Chapter One – I was hooked! Elliott Tepper was saying all that I knew needed to be said to today's Christians. I was thrilled, challenged, encouraged all at once. If you are afraid of another challenge to whole-hearted Christianity, don't buy this book. If you are afraid to step out of a mediocre, half-hearted, divided life-style, don't read this. To be a Christian is to fall in love with Jesus, who gave His all for us, and demands that we give our all for Him. Simple – but costly! Elliott brings this life-style alive for us through many Biblical and living examples. May many Christians get hold of this book and the truth it holds, and allow the Holy Spirit to revolutionise their lives. Thank you, Elliott, for expressing so clearly all that I have longed to shout from the roof-tops!

Helen Roseveare
Former missionary in Congo, internationally respected speaker with WEC ministries and author

THE
COST OF THE
KINGDOM

Elliott Tepper

CHRISTIAN
FOCUS

Copyright © Elliott Tepper 2012
paperback ISBN 978-1-78191-207-2
epub ISBN 978-1-78191-218-8
Mobi ISBN 978-1-78191-221-8

10 9 8 7 6 5 4 3 2 1

First published in 2012 by Amistad Comunicaciones, S.A. de C.

Reprinted in 2013
by
Christian Focus Publications Ltd,
Geanies House, Fearn,
Ross-shire, IV20 1TW, Scotland.
www.christianfocus.com

Cover design
by
Daniel van Straaten

Printed by
Bell and Bain, Glasgow

CONTENTS

Contents

DEDICATION

This book is dedicated to Bob and Catherine Warwick
and Glenn and Nancy Kling,
true citizens of the Kingdom of God.
They have purchased the field, bought the pearl and inspired
generations of disciples to follow in their footsteps.

1

How Much Is a Treasure in a Field Worth?
Ask the Plumber

> Many waters cannot quench love,
> Nor will rivers overflow it;
> If a man were to give all the riches of
> his house for love,
> It would be utterly despised. (Song 8:7)

What is the most-read love poem in world literature? One cannot be certain, but more than likely the Song of Solomon has been read and reread by countless millions of Jews and Christians for almost three millennia. The Song of Solomon or the Song of Songs, for me, is a refuge. I go there when I grow cold and have lost my way. It is there that I often rediscover the ancient path that leads back into the presence of God. It is there that my dry husks of religion are changed into the banqueting house of His Kingdom. As I read and reread familiar passages, meditating on the words of Solomon and the Shulammite professing their love for one another, God always permits me to rediscover His presence. And there He surprises me with His intimate loving kindnesses, while I marvel how I or anyone else could ever forget God's love and the reality of His Kingdom. It is there I discover what the Kingdom of God is about and why men and women throughout the ages have left all to follow Christ.

"He has brought me to his banquet hall, and his banner over me is love" (Song 2:4). The Song of Songs can be read on many levels. We can see the Shulammite and Solomon as lovers who are the archetypes of all lovers. We can also see the celestial Bride and Groom: the Church and Christ, where each praises the beauty of the other. In this song of love, Christ affirms the Church to be a treasure without equal. Not the spiral galaxies, not the cosmos, but we, the Bride of Christ, are His greatest possession. In like manner, the Shulammite declares that Christ is a priceless treasure and not just for her alone, but for all who find Him.

Where does one find incomparable treasures like the King and His Kingdom, Christ and His Church? Treasures are often found in hidden and unfrequented places. Part of their value depends on their rarity and part on their innate quality of being higher and finer than all that surrounds them. The Shulammite is "a lily among the thorns" and the Bridegroom "an apple tree among the trees of the forest."

A Treasure in a Strange Place

Not too long ago I discovered a treasure in a wild and strange place, in Betel of America in New York City. New York is known as the great melting pot where different races and cultures come together to be forged into Americans. I grew up there and know New York well. My father owned businesses in New York City, and I was a student and a competitive athlete. We both knew what it was like to live and struggle in New York. If you are a tourist you may find the city exciting, fascinating, and enchanting, but if you come to live there, you will quickly discover that it is also aggressive, hard, and fiercely proud of being proud. One must fight to survive, and only the tough survive. Perhaps I am being too hard on New Yorkers, but there are real battles every day on their streets and sidewalks. One can feel the press and competitive energy in their stores, offices, schools, playgrounds, and subways. New Yorkers wear their toughness like a badge of honor. I love New Yorkers. I am a New Yorker. But as a missionary, I would like to find a way through that coarse outer veil into their hearts. To be honest, we have found New York City to be one of the most resistant fields in the world to our mission. Billy Graham once said, "To preach the gospel in New York is like digging in granite with a pickaxe."

What treasure did I discover in New York? I met a plumber by the name of Ahmet. Mary and I were visiting our son David, his wife Naomi and their family. They are the directors of Betel of America. Their kitchen drain was blocked, and I decided to unstop it. I took a wire clothes hanger and began to poke into the stopped drain, puncturing the ancient pipe and flooding the kitchen cabinet and the floor. Trying to be helpful, I made a very big mess. David called Ahmet, who had fixed other plumbing problems in the building before. Though it was late, Ahmet came right over. He got down on his knees and then on his side and stuck his head into the cabinet. As he began dismantling the pipes, black, smelly goo poured out onto the floor and onto him. The plumbing was so old that the drainage system broke off right to the wall. It was a bigger problem than we had anticipated, and it was already late.

Ahmet was very cheerful and not discouraged. With gusto he began digging out the black muck that covered him and much of the immediate area under and around the sink. I was struck by his joy and enthusiasm, despite the lateness of the hour and the difficulty and complications he had encountered. The contrast intrigued me. He relished his work and radiated joy. I stayed with him and we talked. I asked him about his family and background. He told me that he came from a Muslim family, but had converted to Christ and was now a member of the Evangel Church of Queens. I asked him what his family thought about his conversion to Christianity. He told me that they did not approve of his new faith. His mother especially was opposed to his conversion and told him that Muslims could not become Christians and would never cease being Muslims.

As we talked, he told me that as a Muslim he had married a Venezuelan evangelical Christian in New York. This was very distressing to his mother, and she had never accepted the fact that he had married a Christian. I asked him if his wife had led him to Christ, and he replied, "No, she did not lead me to Christ." He continued working on his side with his head stuck under the sink, covered in the dirty water and black muck, while he explained to me how he had encountered Christ.

"One day I was sitting alone in the park, totally desolate and in despair. I cried out to God for help and comfort. Then suddenly God filled me with love, overwhelmed me with love, a love that I had never experienced before, in me and around me. And then God spoke to me and asked, 'Do you know my Son?' " Ahmet paused and smiled at me from under the sink with a joy that came from another world. He was like a precious jewel shining in the night. "Of course, even after more than thirty years, my family has never accepted my Christian faith."

The presence of God was very real in the kitchen, and I knew that I was experiencing a transcendent moment in God. I said, "I understand your experience and the reaction of your mother. I am from a Jewish background. In 1971, I cried out to God in Boston with the same agony of heart while walking along the Charles River, and God revealed Christ to me—His love, and Heaven and Hell. My mother would not accept my conversion to Christ and in many ways marginalized me." We both went into more details of our conversion experiences and our Christian lives. Can you see an ex-Muslim plumber lying on the floor covered in black slime with an ex-Jew at his side, both full of light and the glory of God rejoicing in their shared knowledge of Christ? Truly, the Holy Spirit had brought us into His banqueting house, and His banner over us was love.

I said to Ahmet, "It has not been easy, has it, your life and mine, with our families?" His answer surprised me. With a smile he said, "If any man would come after me, let him deny himself, take up his cross each day, and follow me," quoting Luke 9:23. The plumber had gone directly to the heart and core of Christianity and what it means to be a follower of Christ. I cannot imagine a better answer. Ahmet continued, "Now, we have something much better than what we lost." The plumber was simply agreeing with the Carpenter.

In Matthew 13:44 Jesus tells us that "the kingdom of heaven is like a treasure hidden in the field, which a man found and hid again; and from joy over it he goes and sells all that he has and buys that field."

Sometimes I wonder how many Christians who profess Christ have actually found that treasure? We need to ask ourselves: "Have I found something so wonderful and marvelous that I am willing to sell all that I have to buy it?" If what Jesus is asking—giving up everything—sounds strange and excessive and remains a mystery to us, then perhaps we have not yet encountered the treasure.

There are people who believe in the existence of the field and perhaps even have seen and handled the treasure, but they are not willing to sell all to possess it. The price is too high. It is not easy for a young person in the flower of his or her youth to sell all. The attractions of their generation and the approval and praise of their friends are far too important. They simply cannot put all that upon the altar. Then there are the addictive personalities who are simply not willing to sacrifice their temporal pleasures for the eternal treasure. Neither will the man or woman intertwined in an illicit relationship forfeit that relationship to purchase the field. Nor will the individual tied to his wealth and material possessions part with them, whether they are great or small, though he has seen and coveted the good treasure in the field. The list goes on and on. The ranks of humanity are full of men and women who are easily swayed by pressures and temptations of all kinds that give them the excuse for not "selling all that they have" to buy the field.

We can hardly imagine the pressures and the temptations that my friend Ahmet the plumber encountered when he faced his decision to buy or not to buy the field. The forces that Islam can bring against Muslims who convert to Christ are ferocious. The application of Islamic law and discipline varies from Islamic country to Islamic country and among its different sects. On the one hand, Sharia law is brutal. Adultery is punishable by ninety-nine lashes or stoning. Apostasy—conversion from Islam to Christianity—is, according to the Koran, always punishable by death, though the civil law in most Muslim nations would not officially exact the ultimate price. Still, I have heard from a reputable English churchman that in one year, almost all of the Muslim converts to Christianity in his denomination were killed by their own families, either in Great Britain or after being sent back to their home country. Scotland Yard now has a division dedicated to investigating "honor killings" among Muslims.

On the other hand, violations of Islamic moral law and conversion may only be condemned, but without severe civil or family punishment or death. But whether the consequences of conversion to Christianity are absolute or moderate, extreme or measured, conversion is always condemned and frowned upon, and the apostate can expect at minimum ostracism and rejection.

Not infrequently, a softer, but no less insidious approach is tried. The would-be convert is offered many temptations and bribes to return to the fold: a new job, a beautiful new wife, educational opportunities, or whatever will change his or her mind. We can only imagine the pressures, threats, cajoling and perks that Ahmet confronted when he informed his family that he had become a Christian. Surely our trials and temptations are small when compared to his. Still, when a Muslim decides to buy the field with the hidden treasure, he or she knows that the cost may be his or her life.

I have at times wondered why God asks so much from us. I know that God is love and that He is faithful and just and will not allow us to be tempted beyond what we are able to bear. Why do we have to give up everything to obtain the treasure? Why? Because the price is the price, and the price is always all that we have. In Matthew 13:44 the man had no problem with the price. He suffered no "sticker shock." He desired the treasure and believed that it had more value than all that he possessed. With resolve, he took all that he had and bought the treasure with no regret.

Is this too radical? Though it might appear radical to the outward observer, it is the minimum, and the only price that Jesus has ever put upon entrance into His Kingdom, and it is not negotiable. Consider the encounter Jesus had with two men in the tenth chapter of Mark.

The Rich Young Ruler and the Blind Beggar

A man ran up to Him and knelt before Him, and asked Him, "Good Teacher, what shall I do to inherit eternal life?" And Jesus said to him, "… You know the commandments …" And he said to Him, "Teacher, I have kept all these things from my youth up." Looking at him,

Jesus felt a love for him and said to him, "One thing you lack: go and sell all you possess, and give to the poor, and you will have treasure in heaven; and come, follow Me." (Mark 10:17-21)

He went away sad and grieving. That "one thing" was too high a price for that young man to pay. According to Luke's and Mark's accounts, he was rich, powerful, and a governor. Jesus was asking for something he was not able or willing to part with in order to gain the treasure in the field.

The young man essentially said to Jesus: "I do value Your treasure, but my treasure is worth just a little more than Your treasure. I do want to serve and follow You and be part of Your Kingdom, but would You consider *my* conditions? I only have a few and the list is not long; in fact, all I ask is that You let me keep my riches. The reason I suggest that You let me keep my treasure, too, is that together with Your treasure, I will be even better able to serve You." But Jesus was quite clear: "Go and sell all." All is all, and anything less is unacceptable.

For most of us, we do not need to struggle over the decision of whether or not we will abandon all our riches to purchase the field. We have no riches! We must merely decide whether we are willing to sacrifice our humble lives, our broken lives, our sins, self-pity, triumphs, honors, and the few material things we own to buy the field with the treasure.

The price of the field was not specified in the story of The Rich Young Ruler. Why? Perhaps the exact value or content of the price does not matter to the Lord. The conditions of the deal are simple: we give Jesus all that we have, good and bad. Then Jesus gives us the field with the hidden treasure. The rich man and the poor man pay the same: all they have. The beauty of the transaction is that everyone is able to pay the price. Jesus simply asks for everything, no more, no less. Then why do so few accept the offer? Perhaps the real problem is not money or wealth, but other important things. Let me explain.

Also found in the tenth chapter of Mark is the story of the poor, blind beggar named Bartimaeus. Compare the reaction of Bartimaeus to the reaction of the rich young ruler when Bartimaeus discovered the treasure hidden in the field. Jesus had just finished ministering in Jericho, and as He was leaving surrounded by a large crowd, He passed a blind beggar sitting by the road. When Bartimaeus realized that it was Jesus passing by and heard His name on the lips of the crowd, there was something in the name of Jesus that awoke a longing and a hope in his heart. Everything that he had ever wanted was contained in the voice that was resounding within him. Bartimaeus knew in an instant that the fulfillment of all his dreams was approaching. He knew that only the Carpenter could restore his sight.

Bartimaeus cried out, "Jesus, Son of David, have mercy on me!" The crowd tried to silence him and dissuade him from bothering Jesus. The world, religion, even at times the faithful will try to persuade us not to act out of order lest we behave recklessly. They blocked his way. In essence, they were saying, "Who are you to think that a poor blind beggar could merit the Master's attention?" But nothing would discourage him or turn him from his quest. Bartimaeus pressed on against the current of popular opinion, crying louder still, "Son of David have mercy on me!" When Jesus heard Bartimaeus' cry, He stopped and said, "Call him here." Once Bartimaeus knew that he had been heard and called by Jesus, he took courage, stood up and cast off his cloak, his only earthly possession of any value. Jesus beheld the man and said, "What do you want Me to do for you?" And Bartimaeus replied, "Rabboni, I want to regain my sight!" (Mark 10:47-52).

The Scripture clearly indicates that the rich young ruler was good and that Jesus loved him. We do not know much about Bartimaeus, whether he was good or whether he obeyed the Law of Moses. All we know is that he was needy and desperate for God's help. Jesus offered the same treasure to both men and would have accepted either man's currency: the wealth and sincere piety of the young ruler or the dirty rags and broken body of Bartimaeus. Yet only the blind beggar bought the field. Perhaps the true perception of our need and the passionate belief that only Jesus can meet that need are the only qualities that give us the courage to sell all and buy the field. When we see Him for who He is and ourselves for who we are, then we will willingly and with relish exchange our lives and little beggarly fiefdoms for the treasure of His eternal Kingdom. The rich young ruler went away sad, not because he was rich, but because he was not needy enough. Bartimaeus went away full, because he knew he had a need.

Have You Considered My Servant Job?

Let us consider another rich man who one day found himself sitting on the ground, poor, broken and covered with sores and ashes. Job was the richest man of the East during the time of the Patriarchs. He was also godly. If Job were a man of the twenty-first century, he would be the Bill Gates of America, the Amancio Ortega of Spain, or the Carlos Slim of Mexico—someone not just wealthy, but fabulously wealthy.

The story of Job begins, not on the earth, but in the heavenlies. One day Satan dared to appear before the Court of Heaven. God challenged him and asked, "Where have you come from?" Satan replied,

> "From roaming about on the earth and walking around on it." The Lord said to Satan, "Have you considered My servant Job? For there is no one like him on the earth, a blameless and upright man, fearing God and turning away from evil." Then Satan answered the Lord, "Does Job fear God for nothing? Have You not made a hedge about him and his house and all that he has, on every side? You have blessed the work of his hands, and his possessions have increased in the land. But put forth Your hand now and touch all that he has; he will surely curse You to Your face." (Job 1:7-11)

As we read Job's story, up to this point it is very clear that God loved, blessed and protected Job. He was proud of His servant, even boasting before Satan of Job's loyalty and godliness. But how did God respond to Satan's taunt, "touch all that he has; he will surely curse You to Your face"? The Lord allowed Satan to systematically strip Job of everything—his wealth, possessions, servants, children, and friends, even his reputation. When God challenged Satan the second time to consider Job's character, He asked Satan if he had noted that Job "still holds fast his integrity, although you incited Me against him to ruin him without cause" (Job 2:3).

The book of Job is considered to be perhaps the oldest book in the Bible. Job and his story are contemporary to the time of our Father Abraham. This tells me that for over four thousand years, the People of God have wrestled with the meaning of Job's story and suffering. Why does a loving, righteous, all-powerful God allow the righteous to suffer? The answer is hidden in the book of Job and in all of Holy Scripture. I cannot say that I have discovered the answer, but I believe that I have begun to dimly perceive why.

Perhaps it is because God loves us as He loved Job and wants to give us more—a "double portion," a treasure. God wants to give us a deeper, greater revelation of Himself. He wants to enlarge and bless our family and seed. He wants to give us true riches and make us wealthy in all senses of the word. In short, He wants to bring us into His banqueting house.

What did God do for Job and to Job to help the "richest man in the East" understand his need? God made an executive decision for him. He stripped Job of everything but his own life and integrity. I believe God knew that if Job had been asked before his suffering and loss to sell all that he had to buy the field with the hidden treasure, he would have had difficulty putting everything upon the altar. Yet the Lord had confidence in His servant and knew that Job would not ultimately fail to pay the price. In an act of love, God allowed Job to suffer and to be unjustly afflicted by the enemy of men's souls, that Job might desire a higher and greater good.

Have we ever considered that the trials of this life that God permits may actually be acts of God's love? What am I saying? Perhaps the loss of health, riches, family, friends; all the false accusations against us; and the threats against our integrity, perhaps they are the price of the field and the cost of the treasure? Perhaps God is helping us make the payment?

We may not always comprehend the mystery of God's dealings, but we must never doubt His motives. Job's wife did not understand, and she maligned God and mocked Job's integrity and unwavering trust in God. She essentially said, "God is cruel and you are a dupe, an idiot. Get angry at God. Be furious. Curse God and die." How did Job respond? "But he said to her, 'You speak as one of the foolish women speaks. Shall we indeed accept good from God and not accept adversity?' In all this Job did not sin with his lips" (Job 2:10).

We all know the rest of Job's story. Let me recount it in the light of what we have seen in the stories of The Rich Young Ruler and Blind Bartimaeus. Let me put words in Job's mouth: "I have always wanted the field and the treasure, but it was not until God in His love stripped me naked that I became willing to pay all for His field. I have suffered, and I have learned as I journeyed. Now I am prepared to lose, spend, and sacrifice all, that I might gain God and His eternal Kingdom. Though I still do not understand His ways, I know that He is good and loves me. And though I now have nothing to give Him for the field but my broken life, He accepts what little I have left as the price for His great treasure, which is God Himself. Long ago my ears had heard of Him, but now I see Him and count all I have lost as but dust and ashes compared to the treasure that is now mine."

How Much Is a Treasure in a Field Worth?

Ask the plumber and he will tell you what the Carpenter said: "If anyone wishes to come after Me, he must deny himself, and take up his cross daily and follow Me" (Luke 9:23).

There is one price for all. No matter whether you are a Muslim plumber, an American Jew, a rich young ruler, a blind beggar, or the richest man in the old or new world—all must pay all.

Will it be worth it? Ask the plumber again, and he will tell you, "Now we have something much better than what we lost."

2

What Is the True Cost of Discipleship?
Ask the Tax Collector

Jesus made it very clear that all who would be His disciples must renounce all that they have. I believe that the only reasonable response to Jesus' demand, if one has tasted the mystery of the King and His Kingdom, is to pay Him His price and purchase the treasure in the field.

But is entrance into the Kingdom of God that simple and straightforward? Martin Luther once said, if I can paraphrase him from memory: "If the only way to please God is to sell all that you have and give to the poor, then all Christians will be beggars and bankrupts." The logic of Martin Luther's observation agrees with the divergent counsels Jesus gave to different people in the Gospels. His counsel to the rich young ruler simply cannot be universal, but rather particular to that young man's need.

I can remember in my first year on the mission field, walking through a poor Mexican village with an older missionary named Ray Pollnow. A very drunk man came up to me and asked for money. I told him, "No. You will only spend it on drink." He looked at me and said, "If you were a real Christian, you would give me money. Jesus said, 'Give to the poor and you will have treasure in Heaven.'" Taken aback and shamed, I gave him some money, and the man left. Ray turned to me and said, "That is what Jesus said, but not what He meant."

What is the true cost of discipleship? The New Testament tells of many men and women who were very rich and who were also disciples of Christ: Nicodemus, Joseph of Arimathea, some of the principal women of Jerusalem, Cornelius, and many others. Perhaps we need to look more deeply into the correct interpretation of Luke 9:23 and Mark 10:21.

After Jesus instructed the rich young ruler to sell all that he had and to give all to the poor, the young man went away sad. The disciples were dismayed by the heavy demand Jesus placed on the young man. Jesus knew their thoughts, and turned to His disciples and warned them, saying, "How hard it will be for those who are wealthy to enter the Kingdom of God!" They remained perplexed, and Jesus clarified further the meaning of His words. "Children, how hard it is to enter the Kingdom of God! It is easier for a camel to go through the eye of a needle than for a rich man to enter the Kingdom of God." The disciples were still dumbfounded and even more astonished, and said to Him, "'Then who can be saved?' Looking at them,

Jesus said, 'With people it is impossible, but not with God; for all things are possible with God'" (Mark 10:23-27).

Perhaps the demands of Luke 9:23 and Mark 10:21 are simply Jesus asking those who would be His disciples to face a moment of truth in their lives, a moment when they must stand before God totally naked, honest, and humbled, to offer all upon His altar. God knows the heart and accepts all sincere offerings of self and wealth. But once our lives and substance are truly offered and divinely accepted, God then returns all to us and makes us His stewards of our own lives and of what we have. All is His, but now we have become the King's administrators in His Kingdom. And not infrequently, God increases the wealth and social stature of His faithful servants once they have given Him all. As the plumber said, "Now we have something much better than what we lost."

On the Other Side of the Eye of the Needle

Consider the story of Zacchaeus, the chief of the tax collectors and a very rich man, found in the nineteenth chapter of Luke. Jesus had entered Jericho and was passing through on His way to Jerusalem. A multitude surrounded and followed Him as He walked through the city. An inquisitive little man wanted to see the carpenter-rabbi and worker of miracles. He climbed a sycamore tree and waited for Jesus to come into his view. When Jesus came near to Zacchaeus' sycamore, He looked up and said to him, "Zacchaeus, hurry and come down, for today I must stay at your house" (Luke 19:5). Who can imagine what transpired in Zacchaeus' heart in that moment of mutual recognition and new friendship? The despised collector of taxes—a member of that elite group of abusive, covetous, dishonest publicans, the Roman collaborator—was publically declared by Jesus Himself to be His friend.

The curious and adoring multitude that followed Jesus must have been in shock to see Him draw near a rich traitor of so little moral and social consequence. Zacchaeus was not young and handsome like the rich young ruler, but small in stature and only known to the people as the little despised man who sat on the other side of the table behind piles of money collecting their taxes. Yet Jesus discerned something special in the tax collector. Among the multitude of faces, He saw one heart burning brighter than all the others with desire to see and to know the Carpenter.

"Zacchaeus, hurry and come down, for today I must stay at your house." Zacchaeus came down from his tree and received Jesus gladly. Then Zacchaeus did something very bold that must have astounded the multitude and confounded the disciples. He proposed conditions for their new friendship and volunteered to renounce his wealth, or at least a part of it. "Behold, Lord, half of my possessions I will give to the poor, and if I have defrauded anyone of anything, I will give back four times as much" (Luke 19:5-8).

Perhaps the crowd of taxpayers were impressed, but what was Jesus' reaction to Zacchaeus' offer? Did He remind him that in His Kingdom the cost of discipleship was all or nothing? Did Zacchaeus think that he could get off paying less than the rich young ruler, or blind Bartimaeus, or Peter, James and John? Was Zacchaeus daring to make a deal? Instead of rebuke, Jesus loudly proclaimed to the multitude, "Today salvation has come to this house, because he, too, is a son of Abraham. For the Son of Man has come to seek and to save that which was lost" (Luke 19:9-10). Jesus might have replied, "No, not half, but all. There are no exceptions." But He did not. The only conclusion that I can draw is that Jesus is interested in the heart and not in things. Surely what Jesus said to Zacchaeus left both the multitude and the disciples speechless. The multitude must have been greatly impressed by Zacchaeus' reckless and costly gesture of charity and restoration, and Jesus' open-hearted recognition that a sinful publican was indeed a son of Abraham. On the other hand, the disciples must have felt unfairly treated by their Master. Why should the cost of discipleship be all for some and half for others? How did Zacchaeus ever manage to pass through the eye of the needle?

Jesus understood their hearts, and while they stood listening and wondering, He began to more clearly explain the relationship between wealth and discipleship by telling them a parable: "A nobleman went to a distant country to receive a kingdom for himself, and then return. And he called ten of his slaves, and gave them ten minas and said to them, 'Do business with this until I come back'" (Luke 19:12-13).

Jesus told this parable to His disciples in the light of His earlier discourses on wealth and the cost of discipleship with the rich young ruler, Bartimaeus, and Zacchaeus. It was also told in the light of His entry into Jerusalem and His imminent departure to "a distant country" to receive the Kingdom of Heaven. Jesus was telling His disciples that He was going away but would return, and before He left He intended to give to each disciple a measure of minas or talents—wealth with which they were to "do business" until He returned. It is crucial to see that here the nobleman did not ask for a renunciation of wealth from his servants, but rather he placed small fortunes in their hands. Jesus is not some kleptomaniac, not some selfish despot who bleeds his subjects into poverty. He is a generous and noble king who trusts His wealth in the hands of His servants and brethren.

We all know the story—the nobleman returned and asked his servants to give account of what they had done with their talents. Some had greatly multiplied what they had been given, some had multiplied less, and some had hidden what had been entrusted to them and returned their original minas and no more. Each one received their reward according to what they had won for their Lord. In like manner, at the end of the age, we must give account of our stewardship as Christ's disciples. What we have done on earth will determine what we will receive in eternity. Jesus has assured us that if we are faithful now over little, in eternity we will be given authority over much.

If I remember accurately, John Wesley gave this counsel to his early Methodist followers in the eighteenth century: "Earn all that you can. Save all that you can. Invest all that you can. And give away all that you can." It is not important how much you have, but how faithfully you administer what has been given to you in sacred trust by the Master. Once He has established in that moment of truth that all you are and have are His, He returns all and says, "Go now. Do business until I come."

The Lamb Is the Lion

The cost of discipleship is not a one-sided affair. We must not exclusively focus on the cost to the disciple of discipleship, nor overly romanticize the daring risks men have taken to give all to God, as if our sacrifice is of great value. In reality, our sacrifices are not all that heroic, nor altruistic. The Christ who left for a "distant country" will not be the same Christ who will return to judge and reward His servants. In the last days the Lamb will return as the Lion. The Christ who, in His first coming, opened not His mouth, suffering abuse and ridicule, and offering up Himself as a sacrifice for men—that same Christ who paid all will return as a conquering King and will one day judge the living and the dead.

The wise man, who renouncing all to follow Christ today, has not so much offered his all in heroic self-sacrifice, but has merely acted in prudent self-interest. He is no better than the slave who, having served his Master and having done all the things which were commanded, says, "We are unworthy slaves; we have done only that which we ought to have done" (Luke 17:10). He rightly fears God and knows the consequences of withholding his service, worship and homage.

To those who have chosen to give all to God, the Lord has said in the second Psalm, "Ask of Me, and I will surely give the nations as Your inheritance, And the very ends of the earth as Your possession." But to those who have mocked God's claims on man in this life, the psalmist says of the Lord, "You shall break them with a rod of iron, You shall shatter them like earthenware" (Ps. 2:8-9).

The King asks all from His servants and returns all to them with confidence—because He knows that they will be faithful stewards when finally called upon to give account—because they love and fear Him.

3

Where Is the Kingdom?
Ask the Fishermen

Christ is the treasure hidden in the field. How then does the treasure relate to the field? Let me offer a simple definition of the Kingdom of God: The Kingdom of God exists where the King is and where He reigns and governs on earth and in Heaven. The Kingdom of God is then a person and a place—a treasure and a field. It is a place of governance with a King who effectively governs. For us personally, the Kingdom of God is where Christ is our King, and where Christ reigns in us and is obeyed, honored, and worshiped.

The Foundations of the Kingdom
What Scripture in the Bible provides the best foundation upon which to build our understanding of the Kingdom of God? There are many possibilities, but for me Matthew 6 is the best place to begin:

Pray, then, in this way:
"Our Father who is in heaven,
Hallowed be Your name.
Your kingdom come,
Your will be done,
On earth as it is in heaven." (Matt. 6:9-10)

Jesus is teaching His disciples that God reigns in Heaven. He instructs them to pray to the Father that the reign of His celestial Kingdom might come to earth, that the will of His Father and our Father might also be done on earth. God is holy and His reign in Heaven is perfect. Though Satan and his minions may still have access to move about through certain realms of the heavens, they no longer have any authority in High Heaven. Long ago, since before the fall of Adam and Eve, their rebellion had largely been erased from the heavenlies. Jesus said in the Gospel of Luke, "I was watching Satan fall from heaven like lightning." He was citing Isaiah 14:12 which reads:

How you have fallen from heaven,
O star of the morning, son of the dawn!
You have been cut down to the earth,
You who have weakened the nations!

Where has Satan continued his rebellion after being cast out of Heaven? Clearly he has been "cut down to the earth," and it is principally there that he wages his war against God and His Kingdom. Once Satan found himself outside of the Kingdom of Heaven, one of his first conquests on the earth was in the heart of Adam. The whole human race fell in Adam. We understand this today, not just in the light of Scripture, but also in the natural light of science. All our natural and spiritual DNA was in Adam, and we, before the dawn of our own birth or individual consciousness, were all carried captive in his genetic code into another kingdom at war with the Kingdom of God.

Of course, the Devil is not content to merely maintain his rebellion on the earth. He wishes to regain his place in the heavens, and more than that, he fully intends to place his throne above the throne of God: "I will raise my throne above the stars of God, and I will sit on the mount of assembly" (Isa. 14:13).

His strategy was clear. The Devil would first establish his rebellion and kingdom on the earth in the heart of man. Then secondly, once the image of God had been compromised in Adam and his fealty to God broken, once Adam's God-given authority to rule over creation had been usurped by the Devil, the Devil said, if I can interpret his actions into words: "Now that my kingdom has come to earth and to man, let my kingdom come and my will be done in Heaven as it is now done on earth—I will retake my former place and steal God's throne in Heaven."

It is clear. Two kingdoms are contending for Heaven and earth. Two kingdoms are advancing in opposite directions: one from Heaven to earth and one from earth to Heaven. Both wish to re-establish a single kingdom that will reign over both Heaven and earth.

How did God begin His reconquest and the re-establishment of His Kingdom on the earth? He began with the incarnation and sacrifice of Christ: "And the Word became flesh, and dwelt among us, and we saw His glory, glory as of the only begotten from the Father, full of grace and truth" (John 1:14). Jesus, the Word of God, came down from Heaven in order to re-establish His Kingdom on the earth, and His incarnation is the very cornerstone of His Kingdom. That stone is the living stone from which and upon which the entire house is built.

He began in the very place where the Kingdom was lost—in the heart of Adam. The second Adam took the first Adam's place. Through His perfect sinless life, His suffering and sacrifice on the cross, His death and His resurrection, Christ redeemed man to God, pardoning and purifying him, and thus restoring Adam to God's family and Adam's lost kingdom back to God. Christ's incarnation in Jerusalem in the first century began the reconquest, but that reconquest was not limited to a linear timeline from that moment forward in history. We must see that the "Lamb who was slain" was slain before the foundation of the world, so that this mystery of redemption and reconquest would work forward, not just from Calvary, but also from before the beginning of the world to the end of the age.

The Kingdom Is Already In Us and Among Us

What is the second foundation of the Kingdom of God? In Luke chapter 17, the Pharisees asked Jesus when the Kingdom of God would come. Jesus answered them and said, "The kingdom of God is not coming with signs to be observed; nor will they say, 'Look, here it is!' or, 'There it is!' For behold, the kingdom of God is in your midst" (Luke 17:20-21).

The second foundation is also a great mystery. The Kingdom of God already is in us and among us. The Kingdom finds a place first *in* us and *in* every believer through the new birth and regeneration by the Holy Spirit. Then the Kingdom is found *among* us in the Church, which is the Body of Christ, that mystic group of people who share together the mystery in their hearts. More simply put, the Kingdom of God on earth consists of those earthen vessels that together contain the treasure. The earthen vessels are the field, or at least made of the same earth as the field. Then, if we join Matthew 13:44, "The kingdom of heaven is like a treasure hidden in the field," with 2 Corinthians 4:7, "But we have this treasure in earthen vessels, so that the surpassing greatness of the power will be of God and not from ourselves;" it becomes clear that Christ is the treasure and we, the Church, are the field of the parable.

A People for God's Own Possession

Not only are we the field, the Kingdom where the King reigns, but there is yet another mystery, another glory that we must comprehend in the Kingdom of God. Peter tells us that God has made us "a chosen race, a royal priesthood, a holy nation, a people for God's own possession" (1 Pet. 2:9).

I wonder. Do we understand the greatness of our calling in the Kingdom of God? Do we realize that we are to be the nobility of His heavenly Kingdom? We, even now in this life and then for all the ages of eternity, have access to the Father and to His throne. We are part of the royal family. What titles do members of a royal family carry? They are called princes and princesses—heirs to the throne who are called to share the King's power, authority, dominion, and riches. Of course, we are still merely children. This present life is nothing less than our kindergarten, our school, and our university: our field of preparation for eternity. It is the battleground where the mettle and merit of God's mighty men are proven. When I stop for a moment and meditate upon this, I am filled with hope, fear, glorious anticipation and dread, realizing that what I do in this life determines what I will do and be in the Kingdom of Heaven throughout all eternity, worlds without end.

Does all this sound too exaggerated and unreal, a mere projection of our human dreams of grandeur and glory? Why do we doubt that our behavior today might have such wonderful, everlasting consequences? Could it be that our lives and the life of the Church are so dull and reflect so little of the glory, brilliance and nobility of Christ, that we cannot make the connection? Nevertheless, we must hope and believe that we, in our small measure, as we behold the face of Christ, "are being transformed into the same image from glory to glory" (2 Cor. 3:18) by the Spirit of the Lord.

The Gospel and the Acts of Reconquest

We see the Kingdom of God revealed for the first time by Christ in the book of Mark, the shortest and the simplest of the four Gospels. Chapter one paints a clear and concise picture of Jesus and the beginning of His ministry. He is baptized in water by John. Then Jesus is baptized by the Father in the Holy Spirit. Then He is driven by the Holy Spirit into the wilderness to be tempted by the Devil for forty days, to return in power to begin the establishment of the Kingdom of God on the earth. Once John is arrested by Herod, Jesus begins preaching the gospel of the Kingdom of God, saying, "The time is fulfilled, and the Kingdom of God is at hand; repent and believe in the gospel" (Mark 1:15).

The First Act in the Reconquest

The very first act in the Great War to re-establish the Kingdom of God on the earth is Christ Himself preaching the gospel of the Kingdom. Christ came down to earth as a man—as the God-man—to open the first beachhead in this world, declaring that the King and His Kingdom had returned. He went on to say that all men must now choose which king and which kingdom they would serve: God or Satan, God's Kingdom or Satan's kingdom. In Galilee, Christ lifted His voice for the first time before men to say, "Repent; change your allegiance, change your conduct, accept the new King and His dominion."

The Second Act in the Reconquest

Christ wanted more than a beachhead. He wanted the headlands and the valleys, the hills and the mountains, every continent on the whole earth and all who dwell therein. Imagine the invasion of Europe at the end of the Second World War. That invasion began on a single beach on the coast of Normandy in France in 1944. On June 6th, the first Allied soldier stepped onto the beach. Within five days, 356,000 more troops followed that first soldier onto the beaches of Normandy. Before the end of 1945, millions of Allied troops had reconquered all of Europe and utterly stamped out the reign of Hitler wherever it had extended its odious presence on the earth. Christ was the first heavenly warrior to take the first step onto the beachhead of this world in the reconquest of the earth. He immediately invited others to join Him in His warfare:

> As He was going along by the Sea of Galilee, He saw Simon and Andrew, the brother of Simon, casting a net in the sea; for they were fishermen. And Jesus said to them, "Follow Me, and I will make you become fishers of men." Immediately they left their nets and followed Him. Going on a little farther, He saw James the son of Zebedee, and John his brother, who were also in the boat mending nets. Immediately He called them; and they left their father Zebedee in the boat with the hired servants, and went away to follow Him. (Mark 1:16-20)

The first to join Jesus' army of reconquest in the Great War were four fishermen: Simon Peter, Andrew, James, and John. Jesus was quite direct. He simply invited them with an open command that carried no threat, but only a promise to make the fishermen become "fishers of men." That day on the shores of the Sea of Galilee, those four men stepped forward and left their nets, boats, families and friends to become the first citizens and warriors in the Kingdom of God returned to earth. At that moment of submission, and in those first steps of obedience, they had no idea that billions of other men and women would follow their example over the next twenty-one centuries, nor did they realize that the Carpenter King with His little band of Jewish fishermen would one day draw all the Gentile nations into His Kingdom. As they left behind their old lives, they never dreamed that they would proclaim the coming of a new Kingdom so different in kind from all other kingdoms that had ever reigned on earth. Neither did they understand that they would fight a war as no other war had ever been fought before. Surely they could not have imagined that Christ would turn their humble lives into mighty instruments of redemption able to conquer hearts and minds and wills—able to change the loyalty, citizenship, and the destiny of men. They had no idea that they would be the recipients of the Lord's promise to David and Israel in the Second Psalm: "Ask of Me, and I will surely give the nations as Your inheritance, And the very ends of the earth as Your possession."

The Third Act in the Reconquest

What was the third act of reconquest in the Great War? God did wonders again upon the earth. Christ opened the fishermen's eyes to see a demonstration of His power and authority. He wanted His first disciples to see how their war would be waged. Jesus entered a synagogue in Capernaum and began to teach, and the people were amazed:

> For He was teaching them as one having authority, and not as the scribes. Just then there was a man in their synagogue with an unclean spirit; and he cried out, saying, "What business do we have with each other, Jesus of Nazareth? Have You come to destroy us? I know who You are—the Holy One of God!" And Jesus rebuked him, saying, "Be quiet, and come out of him!" Throwing him into convulsions, the unclean spirit cried out with a loud voice and came out of him. They were all amazed, so that they debated among themselves, saying, "What is this? A new teaching with authority! He commands even the unclean spirits, and they obey Him." (Mark 1:22-27)

What exactly happened? Jesus entered a synagogue of the Jews in Capernaum, as was His custom. The Jews were His people and the forerunners, the first sympathizers, of the Kingdom of God on the earth. They were the descendants of Abraham, the "friend of God," who had received the first prophetic promise of the Kingdom of God twenty centuries earlier:

> Now the Lord said to Abram, "Go forth from your country
> And from your relatives and from your father's house,
> To the land which I will show you;
> And I will make you a great nation,
> And I will bless you,
> And make your name great;
> And so you shall be a blessing;
> And I will bless those who bless you,
> And the ones who curse you I will curse.
> And in you all the families of the earth will be blessed."
> (Gen. 12:1-3)

> "Now look toward the heavens, and count the stars, if you are able to count them." And He said to him, "So shall your descendants be." (Gen. 15:5)

Jesus entered into the midst of a congregation of the chosen seed of Abraham and began to preach the coming of the Kingdom of God, the very same Kingdom the Lord had promised to Abraham and his seed in Genesis. They marveled at His teaching because He did not teach as their religious teachers taught. His words were weighty and full of life. His words pulsed with power. The scribes had taught them the old stories and the mighty deeds of

Israel's heroes of faith. But now, standing in their midst, was one who spoke with authority, and they could feel a weight of glory in His words.

How did Jesus demonstrate that His Kingdom, authority and power were more than a mere "idea?" A man with an unclean spirit, a demon, cried out in the midst of the congregation, challenging Jesus' presence and authority. Jesus immediately silenced him and commanded the demon to come out of the man. The man was thrown to the ground in convulsions as the demon cried out and left the man.

How did God end Satan's rebellion in Heaven? He cast Satan out of Heaven. Jesus, the Eternal Logos of God, revealed in Luke 10:18 that He was there in eternity past "watching Satan fall from heaven like lightning." How will God end Satan's rebellion in the earth? In the same way: He will cast Satan out of the earth and out of the hearts of those men who wish to be counted as part of His Kingdom. We too, in this present age, will watch Satan fall from earth as the Eternal Logos re-establishes His dominion in man and over all the earth. Today we must see that deliverance from demonic power is much more than an individual act of deliverance, much more than a noisy evangelistic performance. It is an integral part of God's strategic plan in the Great War of Reconquest.

The Fourth Act in the Reconquest

The fourth act of God's reconquest of earth begins as we read further in the first chapter of Mark, where Jesus took the hand of Simon Peter's mother-in-law. He said nothing but simply took a sick woman's hand, raised her up and healed her. Virtue and power flowed from the King of Heaven back into a daughter of Abraham who had been caught up and afflicted in the Great War between Heaven and Satan's rebellion on earth.

> They came into the house of Simon and Andrew, with James and John. Now Simon's mother-in-law was lying sick with a fever; and immediately they spoke to Jesus about her. And He came to her and raised her up, taking her by the hand, and the fever left her, and she waited on them. When evening came, after the sun had set, they began bringing to Him all who were ill and those who were demon-possessed. And the whole city had gathered at the door. And He healed many who were ill with various diseases, and cast out many demons; and He was not permitting the demons to speak, because they knew who He was. (Mark 1:29-34)

Sickness and infirmity are not of God; neither do they belong in the Kingdom of God. And yet they often afflict the bodies and souls of the redeemed who are the citizens of the Kingdom of God. If sickness exists today on the earth and in the bodies and souls of men and women, its presence is a direct result of the Satanic rebellion brought down to earth and transmitted to man through the fall of Adam in the Garden of Eden. When Adam fell, not only did sin enter the world, but also disease. Though God covered Adam's sin with redemptive sacrifice, thus re-storing his relationship to God, Adam's body remained in a fallen world and subject to all manner of sicknesses and afflictions.

We cannot say when a child of God is sick that it is because they have personally sinned. Perhaps personal sin has caused sickness in some, but many of the righteous suffer simply because they must live and work and walk through a sinful world on their journey into God as they return to their eternal home in Heaven. Some sicknesses are spiritual and some are organic, but at the root, all sickness is the result of the Satanic rebellion and the fall of Adam.

Sickness is an intrusion and an affront to God and man, and it should and can be resisted by faith and the wisdom of God given to man—that is by faith in the power of God to protect and heal, and the efficacy of medicine to assist in the process of healing. It is only right and prudent to trust in God and doctors when one is sick. In the fourth act of reconquest, Jesus dramatically demonstrated to men that He was the Great Physician who had come to deliver all of man—spirit, soul and body—from the devastations of Satan's rebellion and Adam's fall.

The existence of sickness and suffering in the world is among the chief complaints unbelievers lodge against an all-powerful, merciful and loving God. If God were good and if He were almighty, sickness would be banished from the natural order. Their complaint is precisely what Christ's fourth act of reconquest addressed.

God can work much good through sickness and suffering, as we saw in the case of Job. The presence of sickness produced in Job and can produce in us the fruits of patience, mercy, long-suffering, faith and repentance. From Romans 8:28 "we know that God causes all things to work together for good to those who love God," but we also know that all things are not good. They may work together for good. Evil may produce patience in the heart of the righteous. Sickness may produce long-suffering in the afflicted and mercy in the heart of the caregiver, but at rock bottom, sickness is evil and the fruit of the rebellion of Satan and the fall. Jesus, the Great Physician, clearly came to destroy the works of the Devil by publicly and dramatically healing all who were afflicted with disease. "They brought to Him all who were ill, those suffering with various diseases and pains, demoniacs, epileptics, paralytics; and He healed them" (Matt. 4:24).

If I may speak from personal experience, I see the infirmities, tragedies, and sufferings our family has experienced through the years not caused by sin in ourselves, nor by the inattention or cruelty of God, but rather because we are clay pots in the midst of the Great War—a spiritual war of cosmic dimensions between God and the Devil, good and evil, angels and demons—two kingdoms with all their citizens and denizens locked in battle. We are each in our measure caught in the flow of battle.

The Kingdom Has Suffered Violence

Adam might have lost his kingdom and dominion, but from before the foundation of the world, God the Father willed that His Son would win it back for God and man. That Great War has raged from Adam to Noah, from Abraham to Moses, from John the Baptist, the last of the prophets of the Abrahamic Covenant, until the present age of the Church. God has not hidden that war would be costly from those who have pledged their allegiance to the King of Heaven. They have often had to say like Job, one of God's earliest soldiers, "Though he slay me, yet will

I trust in him" (Job 13:15 KJV). They have always been called to leave their nets and boats, families and ambitions on the beachheads of this world to follow their Captain and King into battle. He has never hidden the blood and the violence of the campaign from His comrades but has openly invited them to join in the final reconquest of the nations.

"The kingdom of Heaven suffers violence, and violent men take it by force" (Matt. 11:12). Will it be worth it? All the pain and suffering, trials and privations? Ask the first Jewish fishermen who followed Him. History testifies that through their lives and sufferings, they preached the gospel of the Kingdom and built His Church. They won their crowns as He won His crown. Worldly kings may have their crowns of jewels and gold, but Jesus chose a crown of thorns and tears, and for this, the Father has made Him King of Kings forever. The humble band of men who followed Him also "loved not their lives unto the death" (Rev. 12:11 KJV). They counted the cost and chose the better part.

4

The Details in the Greater Picture

The prophets saw through a glass darkly and left us hints of the coming Kingdom. Later, Jesus spoke both in parables and then directly and clearly of the arrival and final triumph of the Kingdom of God on earth. Today, thanks to the light of the prophets, Jesus, the apostles, and the early Fathers of the Church, we know the trajectory and destiny of the King, His Kingdom, and those who belong to Him. We have been given much light. How can we succinctly describe the coming of the Kingdom that God is re-establishing in the hearts of men?

We must begin with Christ Himself coming down from Heaven to declare, "the Kingdom of Heaven is at hand," followed by His invitation to all men to join Him as soldiers in His Great Crusade of reconquest. From the beginning, He made it very clear that His demands of discipleship and service were absolute. He knows the heart of man and whether our professed loyalty and sacrifices are pure and true. He knows if our all is truly all. He has warned us that the battles will be fierce and that each one of us will be caught in the midst of the fighting. Finally, He has promised that the victory is certain and the future rewards well worth whatever sacrifices we are called to make. That is the big picture, and I think that most Christians would agree to this simple outline.

And They All Lived Happily Ever After

In his classic essay "On Fairy Stories," J. R. R. Tolkien said that he believed the Christian story to be true: the fall of man, the incarnation of Christ, His life, His death, His resurrection and the final redemption of man. Tolkien believed that, in the end, all of human history will turn out to be His Great Story and will end like all true fairy tales, "and they all lived happily ever after." He coined a new word to describe how everything will suddenly be "turned right." He called the sacrifice of Christ, His death and His resurrection the great "Eucatastrophe"—the good catastrophe, the sudden setting right of what had been cast down.

For me, and I think for many other Christians, we are willing to sell all and buy the field because we believe that the story of redemption does have a happy ending. We believe that Christ has told us a true story, and no matter how many twists and turns there may be in the plot and action, that all will turn out just as He promised, and we will all live happily ever after.

I remember the day I chose Christ and His Kingdom. "He brought me into His banqueting house" and gave me a glimpse of Himself and our eternal home. I knew from that moment that if I chose Him and His Kingdom, I would be able to say, like Julian of Norwich: "All shall be well, and all manner of things shall be well." I hesitated a little, but made my choice believing in a certain and happy ending. That was forty years ago. Despite having passed through my share of life's bitter trials, I still believe in the happy ending.

The Devil Is in the Details

When a Christian decides to follow Christ as a disciple, he immediately is faced with two difficulties that perplex and confound him. God has opened our spiritual eyes, and we have grasped the big picture. We have made the right choice, renouncing all to follow Christ. We believe that the big picture is true, yet there are two sticky details that throw sand on the axle of our chariot as we journey towards His and our gloriously happy ending.

First, most of the big picture is still in the future. We cannot understand how our personal struggles of faith can possibly be relevant to or affect His grand design for the ages.

Secondly, as individuals, we are still stuck in the details of our particular moment in the big picture. What is happening to us and to our family today seems of far greater importance than what will happen 100 or 1,000 years in the future, when God unfolds His plan and His happy ending. We are even so short-sighted that what happens today in our lives looms with far greater importance than our own happy ending ten, twenty, or thirty years in the future. We cannot hear Jesus when He says to us, "Let not your heart be troubled. Each day has enough trouble of its own. Only believe." The hope of one day hearing Jesus say, "Well done my good and faithful servant," seems of little present comfort.

Sometimes the details are so painful that we feel as if we are no more than a doormat to be stepped upon, a place where the other protagonists in God's plan clean their boots. We are like the Polish peasants who have been trampled upon time and again by the great armies of Europe: by Napoleon and the czars of Russia, or most recently, by Hitler and Stalin. Through a quirk of geography and no fault of the Polish people, the great powers of the West and the East have turned their land into someone else's battlefield. They are merely a small nation caught in the middle of the great wars between great powers. How many times has little Israel been trampled upon by the great armies of the ancient world: Egypt, Assyria, Babylon, Persia, Greece, and Rome, merely because their lives and real estate were the battlefield where the conflicting powers clashed, fought, and passed through?

Kings, Generals, Soldiers and Peasants

It is one thing to plan and observe a war as a king with his generals, moving colored blocks and pins and flags over large maps and screens. It is quite another thing to be poor peasants, watching their homes being burned and their sons bleeding in the trenches they were commanded to dig by the generals who do not even know their names and are far from the actual conflict. The generals may be honorably doing their part to win a just war, but from the peasant's perspective his response is, "I am nothing more than a farmer. All I want is to live in peace. But your armies continually criss-cross and crush my crops. Again and again you burn our homes and barns, conscript our sons, and drive our family, friends and neighbors away. Why can't you just leave us in peace? It is your war, not ours."

Is not this how the big picture of the struggle to establish the Kingdom of God on earth appears to affect our personal lives? From our personal perspective, we simply cannot understand the necessity of the details in the conduct of the great spiritual war waging around us. It is not enough to say, "Suffer now and you will receive glory later," or "Remember, all things will work together for good for those who love God." In our moment in history, it is very difficult to comprehend the necessity of our personal sacrifices and trials in the greater struggle.

On another level, our inability to comprehend the part our personal sufferings play in our own greater good and the greater good God has planned for man is like trying to explain the joys of homework, school, grammar, and exams to adolescents—explaining that one day, if they endure, they will understand the joys and depths of Cervantes and Shakespeare, or, if they study mathematics and science now, one day they will be able to build or buy a house, fix or buy a car, practice medicine and heal the sick, or manage a business. Perhaps their parents understand, but from the perspective of the adolescent stuck in the details and pains of homework and exams, it makes no sense. Any reasonable young person can only conclude that the adult world's demands on his life are cruel and absurd. This is, of course, the wrong conclusion, but one that most unbelievers and even many Christians draw from the events that affect their lives.

I do not want to insinuate that God is cruel and absurd, or that many Christians act like adolescents, or imply that God is only interested in the big picture and is insensitive to the painful details of our daily lives. The truth is, in fact, quite the contrary. In the incarnation of Christ, God has tenderly drawn His own life together with our personal lives and sufferings into the big picture. When the Logos became flesh to dwell among us, the triune God decided to make the reconquest of earth very personal—not just for men, but also for Himself. The great transcendent and omnipotent God made Himself small and vulnerable, to enter into the sufferings of those who are small and weak. He did not remain above, directing the Great War between powers and principalities, heavenly angels and fallen angels, but He dressed Himself in flesh and came down to live and die in the trenches with us. How different is the God of Abraham, Isaac, and Jacob, and His Christ, from the arrogant gods of the Greco-Roman pantheon who peered down from Olympus upon men. If they entered men's lives, it was only to toy with them in fickle delight or callous wrath. How intimate are the Son of Man's sufferings for man when compared to Allah's cold indifference and aloof, unbridgeable separation from the human race. Without doubt, Isaiah identified the cardinal difference between Christianity and all other religions:

> Surely our griefs He Himself bore,
> And our sorrows He carried;

But He was pierced through for our transgressions,
He was crushed for our iniquities;
The chastening for our well-being fell upon Him,
And by His scourging we are healed.

But the Lord was pleased
To crush Him, putting Him to grief;
If He would render Himself as a guilt offering,
He will see His offspring,
He will prolong His days,
And the good pleasure of the Lord will prosper in His hand.
(Isa. 53:4, 5, 10)

In Isaiah 53, clearly God chose to involve Himself in the individual, existential details of the big picture by becoming a man. The destiny of all of humanity and the weight of redemptive history fell upon that single Life that chose to live as men live.

Early in World War I, in 1915, Great Britain suffered one of its greatest defeats and military tragedies on the shores of Gallipoli in Turkey. By the time the British had withdrawn from Gallipoli in 1916, they had suffered more than 500,000 casualties. Winston Churchill, as the First Lord of the Admiralty, left his command room in London where its walls and tables were covered with maps and colored blocks and little flags. He stepped down from his high place of power where he had directed the invasion safely from afar and assumed full responsibility for the defeat and the personal suffering of the failed invasion. He resigned as the Lord of the Admiralty and enlisted as a soldier to serve with the British Army in the trench warfare of northern Europe. His heroic gesture was but a shadow of the self-emptying and identification Christ experienced when He left His throne in Heaven to become a man and make Himself a sacrifice for our sins.

Christ "emptied Himself, taking the form of a bond-servant, and being made in the likeness of men. Being found in appearance as a man, He humbled Himself by becoming obedient to the point of death, even death on a cross" (Phil. 2:7-8).

Let us take heart and not wince or whine when the costs of the Kingdom seem heavier than we can bear. We must remember, "Since we have a great high priest who has passed through the heavens, Jesus the Son of God, let us hold fast our confession. For we do not have a high priest who cannot sympathize with our weaknesses, but One who has been tempted in all things as we are, yet without sin" (Heb. 4:14-15).

Lead Me to the Rock That Is Higher Than I

Let us consider the story of a little person called to be part of God's grand design in His war of reconquest and the building of His Kingdom on the earth. I am thinking of a certain humble pastor—David, the son of Jesse.

David was called by God to be the future king of Israel and the patriarch and founder of a messianic line of kings, which would one day bring forth from their loins the Seed of David, Jesus Christ the Messiah. The little pastor was destined to be the beloved of God, the sweet psalmist of Israel, whose songs of worship, whose tears of grief, and whose ecstasies of joy would echo in the heart of Israel for more than a hundred generations. This was the big picture and his calling as God painted it. However, for much of David's life, the reality of being stuck in the details of personal affliction, rejection, persecution, and the sufferings caused by the chaff of his own sins seemed a truer picture. From David's psalms, we know that often he almost lost hope when the sting and pain of the details clouded his understanding and weakened his faith in God's promise to fulfill His Word.

Consider Psalm 18 and its context in the life of David and the plan of God for David and Israel. As we read this psalm, we know that David had already been anointed by the prophet Samuel to be the future king of Israel. Samuel had already publicly declared the will of God: God would take the kingdom of Israel from Saul and would give it to a better man, to David. On that day when Samuel poured out the anointing oil upon David's head, while God's call to kingship covered and penetrated his very being, I am sure David glimpsed in an instant both his and Israel's happy ending. That glimpse and other glimpses were often the only hope that David possessed to sustain him as he walked out his part in God's plan for him and for Israel.

Saul had not accepted the prophet's word, but rather he clung to his own kingdom. After David's victory over Goliath, Saul promoted David and took him into his court, but David's fame and popularity quickened the seeds of jealousy in Saul's heart. He repeatedly threatened David's life, finally forcing him to flee into the wilderness. It was there in the desert of Israel that David wrote many of his most beloved psalms, and there where he gathered his followers who would become the soldiers and first citizens in the new kingdom God had promised to raise up through the obscure shepherd boy.

Psalm 18 begins with David and his small band of men pursued by Saul and his army in the wilderness of Judah, driven to take refuge in a great rock. He is surrounded by Saul's army and trapped in a desperate defense with no hope of escape. It is never good to make one's last stand on a rock in the desert without water, food, or shelter, and no way of escape. It is never good to be trapped on a rock—unless that Rock is the Lord. For if that Rock is the Lord, then there is no better place and no safer place to be in the whole universe, though one is surrounded by human and demonic hosts.

David's situation was desperate. As the human army of Saul pressed upon his last stronghold, in the realm of the spirit, the cords and snares of death also were tightening around his life like torrents of ungodliness, dragging him down into Sheol. What did David do in his last hopeless stand? He declared his love directly to God, "I love You, O Lord, my strength." David did not try to explain the situation. He did not try to educate God concerning the details of his suffering. He simply cried out and declared his love.

I remember, about twenty-five years ago, our sons were playing on the chin-up bar I had put in the doorway of their bedroom. Our second son Jonathan was nine years old. As he swung on the bar he lost his grip and fell on his head. He fell with such force that I can still hear the terrible sound of his head hitting the hard tile floor. My first thought was, "O God, he has died!" Before I could pick him up in my arms, he shouted, "I love you, Daddy!" In Psalm 18, an army of men and the legions of death surrounded young David. He was without human hope. But he, too, cried out to his Father, "I love You, O Lord, my strength." What father will not hear and answer his son when he cries out to him? All good fathers hear their sons and will answer. How much more will our Heavenly Father hear us, and not only hear, but act on our behalf. The Father will move Heaven and earth to save His sons and daughters.

And my cry for help before Him came into His ears.

Then the earth shook and quaked;
And the foundations of the mountains were trembling
And were shaken, because He was angry.

He bowed the heavens also, and came down
With thick darkness under His feet.

He sent out His arrows, and scattered them,
And lightning flashes in abundance, and routed them.

He sent from on high, He took me;
He drew me out of many waters.
He delivered me from my strong enemy,
And from those who hated me, for they were too mighty
for me. (Ps. 18:6, 7, 9, 14, 16, 17)

When we are overwhelmed by the details of our personal struggles in our small role in God's Grand Design for the Ages, let us take heart. The God of Israel hears those who love Him and will shake Heaven and earth for their sake. The Most High, who uttered His voice and manifested His might over nature and angelic powers to deliver David, will do the same for all who love Him, in all generations.

When we are mired in the details, let us not lose sight of the importance God places upon our well-being. We must remember that our little lives are part of a bigger theater of action, a theater of reality God controls, where the seen and the unseen work together for us as the Great War of Reconquest rages in us, around us, and above us. Every part is important to the whole.

Those Who Are With Us Are More Than Those Who Are With Them

We see that theater of the seen and unseen with even greater clarity in the sixth chapter of 2 Kings. Elisha and his servant were surrounded and trapped in the city of Dothan by the army of the King of Syria. Early in the morning the servant awoke to see the army of Syria besieging the city. He cried out to Elisha, "Alas, my master! What shall we do?" Like David, they were trapped on a rock with no human hope of escape. Then Elisha answered him, "Do not fear, for those who are with us are more than those who are with them." And he prayed, "'O Lord, I pray, open his eyes that he may see.' And the Lord opened the servant's eyes and he saw; and behold the mountain was full of horses and chariots of fire all around Elisha" (2 Kings 6:15-17).

When the big picture and grand design of God seem so far away and unrelated to our personal plight, we must remember that we are part of that big picture which surrounds us, envelops us, and ultimately protects us, though we do not perceive it with our natural senses. We may have to wait for deliverance. We may cry out in despair as Jesus cried on the cross, "My God, My God, why have You forsaken Me?" But the same multitude of the heavenly host that surrounded Joseph, Mary and

Jesus at His birth, though unseen by men, was also there at Calvary. Suddenly, at any moment, they may appear to us as they suddenly appeared to the shepherds in Bethlehem. Though at times we are seemingly overwhelmed, we can be as certain of our own happy ending as Christ was of His own resurrection.

What Do We Do While We Wait?

God will not only rescue and set us free from our enemies in the great spiritual war that rages around us, but He will also do many other things for us while we wait upon our King. We have sold everything to purchase the field. The treasure is now ours. We believe in the happy ending that the Lord has purposed for our life in the ages to come. His grace has fortified us to face with courage the details of our minor walk-on part, in our small scene in His great play. But what do we do while we wait and watch and serve in our little outpost as the other principal actors take the center stage?

I believe that there are recompenses all along the way, and that God does not intend for us to wait empty-handed and in vain. When David was trapped upon the desert rock and surrounded by Saul's army, though it appeared that all hope of escape had collapsed, God visited him and opened a secret door. In that very day of his calamity, David could say, "He brought me forth also into a broad place; He rescued me, because He delighted in me" (Ps. 18:19). The testimony of Scripture and of the saints throughout the ages reveals that God opens broad places of inner wonder and beauty to those who love Him, even before whatever actual deliverance may or may not occur. These intimate insights and revelations of His eternal Kingdom sustain us. They are broad, deep seas of fellowship and communion.

I remember reading Richard Wurmbrand's *Tortured For Christ* with amazement when I was a young missionary in Mexico. He was the leader of the Lutheran Church in Romania and the communists had made him the principal public scapegoat and focus of the communist persecution of the Romanian Church. In his story, he recounts that his greatest fear and dread was that of being suddenly delivered from his captivity and torture. One might ask, "How can that possibly be?" He was not a masochist. Certainly he wanted to be free? Wurmbrand simply put what he had lost and what he had gained in the balance. Even in his darkest hours of torture and isolation, he described how the walls of his cell glowed and were transparent like diamonds. He dreaded exchanging the broad open fields of delight and revelation that God had set before him in the Spirit during his temporal captivity for mere physical freedom. Like David the shepherd, and Ahmet the plumber, he was sustained by the knowledge that he had "gained something much better than what he had lost."

Once we discover the mystery of God, we can sing with David:

> For who is God, but the Lord?
> And who is a rock, except our God,
> The God who girds me with strength
> And makes my way blameless?
> He makes my feet like hinds' feet,
> And sets me upon my high places. (Ps. 18:31-33)

He will place us in a broad place and give us faith, revelation, and divine imagination that we might rise up with hinds' feet to the heights of Zion, to leap from mountain to mountain, from precipice to precipice of wonder and glory, to discover the inner world of the Spirit—a world whose horizon has no end.

Behold That Dreamer Cometh: A Soldier Who Never Fought

When the costs of the Kingdom seem too much to bear, take comfort. God will give more to those who are exposed to the greatest risk. The axiom is this: "As thy days, so shall thy strength be" (Deut. 33:25 KJV). It is true. The greater the risk, the greater the divine support, and ultimately, the greater the prize will be in eternity. The bravest and most trusted soldiers are exposed to greater stress and danger than those of lesser strength and loyalty. Why? Because their Captain knows that they will neither faint nor fail in the heat of battle. God leaves the valiant in the most exposed advanced posts, surrounded by enemies, where they will stand and fight though all hope seems lost.

One of God's most illustrious warriors in the Great War of Reconquest was a soldier who never fought. I am thinking of Joseph, the son of Jacob. Joseph was Jacob's favored son, the son who received the coat of many colors. He was gifted by God to dream dreams and destined to be the leader and savior of his people and of ancient Egypt. That was the big picture. However, a deep pit and many years of suffering and injustice rose up before him, blurring and almost blotting out whatever sense Joseph had of his higher calling and destiny.

Where David and his band of followers fought their last desperate defense on a desert rock, and Elisha and his servant took refuge behind the high walls of the city of Dothan, Joseph was called to take his last stand alone in a dark pit also near Dothan. He had neither a warrior's sword nor a city's walls with which to defend himself, but rather as a defenseless, innocent victim, he was thrown into a hole to await his fate. From that ignoble pit, his cruel and jealous brothers sold him into slavery. Though God's hand and favor remained upon his life, favor and honor always seemed to be followed by betrayal. He was favored by his father but betrayed by his brothers, favored by Potiphar but betrayed by Potiphar's wife, and finally, favored in prison only to be betrayed and forgotten by the baker. Despite God blessing Joseph's life with so many tantalizing deliverances and advancements—all of which seemed to place Joseph's destiny almost within his reach—again and again, all was snatched away by the evil in the hearts of others. Yet, Joseph never fainted at his post in the Great War but waited faithfully on God. His willingness to embrace the costs of the Kingdom of God with long-suffering made him truly great in God's sight and a great deliverer for his people.

When nasty details and disappointments cloud our vision, let us remember that there is only one big picture and that God has made us all, in our small way, a part of that story. Only God knows what each man or woman must and can bear. We can be sure that He will be kind and only put upon us what is good and right, and what will make us one day worthy to take our place in that great, final happy ending. Joseph could not have managed a better ending to his story even if he had been allowed to write it himself. Neither can we. It is all of grace and it is His doing.

Let us not think either too much or too little of ourselves, or of our small part in His play. Or, as Gandalf said to Bilbo Baggins:

> Surely you don't disbelieve the prophecies, because you helped bring them about? You don't really suppose, do you, that all your adventures and escapes were managed by mere luck, just for your sole benefit? You're a fine person, Mr Baggins, and I'm very fond of you; but you're only quite a little fellow in a wide world, after all!" (*The Hobbit* by J. R. R. Tolkien)

5

Divine Prosperity
A Cost-Benefit Analysis

A few years ago, Brian Huston traveled to Spain to visit missionaries who were related to the Hillsong Church of Sydney, Australia. Those missionaries engaged our Betel auditorium in Madrid for a special conference and platform for his ministry. Everything associated with the event was edifying and in good taste, a blessing. I, personally, was enlarged and enriched by the humility and authenticity of Brian's life and ministry. During one of the evening meetings, I was sitting in the first row in front of the platform alongside of Brian. In the middle of the worship, Brian turned to me and said, "Betel is different than other Spanish churches we have visited. The evangelical Spanish Church seems to have a spirit of poverty. Betel does not. Betel has a spirit of prosperity." He paused and then asked, "Why?"

There was no criticism in Brian's comment, but a simple observation. In those few moments I took to reply, I thought, "Yes, most Spanish evangelical churches are poor. Most are located in small storefronts with humble, working-class and immigrant congregations. Most have cement or tile floors and folding chairs." I thought, "We started like that, too." My eye studied some of the familiar faces of our own working-class, immigrant, and ex-addict congregation. Then I looked around at Betel's large auditorium that seats more than a thousand people, with its blue carpet and soft chairs, its three-story ceiling and stained-glass windows.

As I gazed around, the brilliant colors of the flags of the nations where Betel has established communities and churches around the world seemed to leap off and accent the tall, white walls of the auditorium. Just before I answered, my eye was drawn to the rich blond oak table and pulpit that Bernardo, Alberto's father, had made for Betel. Bernardo, himself a former alcoholic, was the first father of an addict, who, along with his son, had been converted in Betel. I remembered Bernardo asking me, "What verse would you have me carve on the front of the table?" I replied, "Put John 12:21, 'Sir, we would see Jesus.' Let that always be before the congregation."

Brian was still looking at me and waiting when finally I replied, "I suppose it is because we work with poor people." He smiled and nodded his head.

Sir, We Would See Jesus

Prosperity—is it good? Is it bad? What is prosperity? Has the humble Carpenter, who was a friend of the poor and has asked for costly sacrifice from His disciples, found a place for prosperity in the Kingdom of God? Before I address these questions, let me share another anecdote that will help explain what I understand divine prosperity to be and what place it has in the Kingdom and councils of God.

Recently, I was asked to speak at the dedication of a small church building in Andalusia. I was not the only speaker. The missionary who founded the church had also invited an elder from his home church in Virginia to speak at the dedication. The elder and I had never met before, but we soon discovered that our paths had indeed crossed. In the early 1970s, we both attended a small church called Seagate Community Chapel in Wilmington, North Carolina. In 1974, Mary and I had left Wilmington to enter Elim Bible Institute to prepare for the mission field just as he and his wife arrived in Wilmington. Though we physically missed each other by only a few months, we knew the same people and had been the beneficiaries of the same deep teachings. In short, we had both spent rich times of fellowship at Seagate Chapel, in the same deeper-life, Charismatic-Pentecostal church.

In the early days of the Charismatic movement, most Charismatics were still active in their mainline denominations, but they also sought fellowship and teaching beyond their home churches in Christian organizations like Camps Farthest Out, the Full Gospel Businessmen, Women's Aglow, World Map Camps, etc. The little Seagate Chapel became, for a short season, a special place of encounter for the embryonic and growing Charismatic movement in Wilmington and the surrounding areas. Many of the best-known and most articulate Charismatic speakers came to minister at Seagate: men like Derek Prince, Bob Mumford, DeVern Fromke, Costa Deir, A. S. Worley, and so many others whose names were household words for anyone who subscribed to the *New Wine* or *Charisma* magazines. For a short season, hungry seekers after the deep things of God were meeting seven days a week in that little chapel. Some of the meetings were so powerful that Seagate Chapel's fame spread far beyond Wilmington. For a season, there seemed to rest upon that little church a similar mantle and a small measure of the blessing that rested on Azusa Street in Los Angeles in the early 1900s.

The elder from Virginia had moved away from Wilmington in the late 1970s. We finished our Bible school training in 1977 and left America in 1978 for the mission field. Wilmington was still our home base, and we returned regularly to visit family and friends. The elder from Virginia then asked me, "How is Seagate doing today?" After all our reminiscing over the past glories of Seagate's golden age of Charismatic visitation, my answer stunned both my new friend and me. I replied, "Seagate hardly exists anymore. The chapel is still standing, but there are only a few old faithful brethren left in an empty building." He replied, "How can that possibly be? So many people were touched and transformed by God there!" I was not sure what to say and then said, "I think I know why. After a number of good pastors, a flashy 'super-faith prosperity' preacher destroyed the church." That statement just came out of my mouth. I had not thought deeply about it, but once said, it rang true. The emphasis that man had placed on the "gospel of prosperity" had replaced the mantle of glory that had rested for so many years on Seagate's congregation. I am sure Seagate's decline was much more nuanced than my spontaneous response, but that is what I said.

What Is Prosperity?
The definitive word of Scripture on prosperity is found in 3 John 1:1-4 which reads:

> The elder to the beloved Gaius, whom I love in truth. Beloved, I pray that in all respects you may prosper and be in good health, just as your soul prospers. For I was very glad when brethren came and testified to your truth, that is, how you are walking in truth. I have no greater joy than this, to hear of my children walking in the truth.

Why did the Apostle John rejoice? He was pleased with his children. He had heard from the brethren that his spiritual children walked in the truth and that they gave witness to the truth. John wanted them to know that he took pleasure in hearing that the truth of the Logos was lived out in their lives and that they willingly shared that Logos with the world. In these opening verses of his epistle, John essentially praised the spiritual quality of their lives.

And yet it is telling; he was also evidently concerned about the quality of their natural lives. The preamble to his rejoicing in their spiritual progress is a simple prayer for their personal well-being: "I pray that in all respects you may prosper and be in good health, just as your soul prospers."

What was the earnest desire of John, their spiritual father, and the will of God for them? Divine prosperity in all the dimensions of life. I would say that his prayer also reflects my desire for my natural and spiritual children in the Tepper and Betel families.

What normal people, what well-balanced human beings, would not desire the blessings of prosperity mentioned in 3 John for the lives of those they love? Suppose we were to select a group of Christians at random and then put the question to a vote: Who would be poor and who would be prosperous? I would be the first to vote for prosperity. Every pastor has prayed the Apostle John's prayer for his own family and congregation. Under normal circumstances, can you imagine a pastor praying the blessings of poverty and suffering over those he loves? Something like this, "Beloved, I desire that you might be poor and enjoy the fruits of poverty in all things—trials, tribulations, hunger, needs, sicknesses, and rejection, all in order that you might become holy."

No pastor would pray a prayer like that today, at least not under normal circumstances. I say under "normal circumstances" because, if one knows anything about the history of the Church and Christian mysticism and asceticism, there have been times when godly men and women in the Church indeed prayed prayers like that and willingly sought after and embraced lives of poverty and suffering.

The Desert Fathers

At the beginning of the third century of the Christian era, there arose in the Church of Egypt a significant group of earnest Christians called the Desert Fathers. Thousands of men and women left their churches in the cities to go to the desert to become hermits, monks, and mystics, seeking union with Christ through abnegation of self, renunciation of the world, extreme asceticism, and sacrifice. They chose Jesus' first challenge to the early disciples as the foundation of their call to discipleship:

> "If anyone wishes to come after Me, he must deny himself, and take up his cross and follow Me. For whoever wishes to save his life will lose it; but whoever loses his life for My sake will find it." (Matt. 16:24-25)

and

> "If you wish to be complete, go and sell your possessions and give to the poor, and you will have treasure in heaven; and come, follow Me." (Matt. 19:21)

Though Jesus Himself lived among men and celebrated life, eating and drinking and attending weddings, the Desert Fathers chose a life not unlike John the Baptist's in the desert. Why they chose to follow John's solitary approach to holiness rather than Jesus' more balanced walk among men, punctuated by short seasons of solitude in desert places, we do not know. Perhaps after the Roman world made peace with the Church in A.D. 313 and ended Rome's official persecution of Christians, many Christians felt that the world had not really ceased in its hostility, but had only changed its tactics. Where before Rome was a raging lion tearing the Church apart, after Constantine's edict of acceptance, Rome became a smothering bear crushing the Church in its worldly embrace. The Desert Fathers saw the self-denial of extreme asceticism as an alternative to martyrdom and a way of preserving the holiness and purity of true Christian discipleship in a Church drifting into the arms of the world.

Streams of this *via negativa* and extreme asceticism have remained within the Church throughout its long history up until today. It has always produced a mixture of holiness and fanaticism, great saints and tragic fanatics. During the Middle Ages, the Catholic, Orthodox, and Coptic churches gave birth to many healthy and unhealthy ascetic communities. Modern Catholics still have their Carthusian and Trappist monks, closed convents, and Mother Teresas. Evangelicals have their William Booths and his humble army of Salvationists, and many other streams of austere Pietists and Holiness Christians. Even in my own mission, WEC International, we embrace the ethos and example of our founder, C. T. Studd. He was born into a millionaire family and yet gave away his inheritance in a single day to follow Christ's admonition in Matthew 19:21 to the letter. He and his wife Priscilla agreed to a sixteen-year separation beginning in 1913, when she ran the home base in London while he lived and preached the gospel in the heart of Africa. Stewart Dinnen, a former international director of WEC, helped collect many of C. T. Studd's sayings found in a little book edited by Jean Walker called *Fool and Fanatic*. I remember a conversation we had one day while we were traveling through the south of Spain visiting the Betel communities to gather material for Betel's story, "Rescue Shop Within a yard of Hell". Stewart asked the question, "Was C. T. Studd a fanatic?" And before I could answer, he answered his own question, "Yes, he was a fanatic, but he was God's fanatic." We modern WECCERS live today, though certainly imperfectly, by what C. T. Studd wrote in a note to his wife shortly before sailing from Europe to Africa: "If Jesus Christ be God and died for me, then no sacrifice can be too great for me to make for Him."

I believe that most of the historic Christian ascetics, mystics, and practitioners of voluntary poverty and self-denial did what they did because they sought union with Christ. That was their stated aim. How can we know or question their motives? Some found union and some did not. Asceticism in any age will always produce a brilliant mixture of fanaticism and, or, true holiness which only God can sort out.

The Way of Affirmation

There is another way. For the vast majority of Christians, God has called us not in the way of Christian asceticism or the *via negativa*, but rather in the *way of affirmation* so clearly stated by the Apostle John, "Beloved, I pray that in all respects you may prosper and be in good health, just as your soul prospers" (3 John 1:2).

Yet even in the *way of affirmation*, prosperity is not always strictly prosperity and good health. That way will always contain a measure of Luke 9:23, which states, "If anyone wishes to come after Me, he must deny himself, and take up his cross daily and follow Me." Right in the middle of the *way of affirmation*, all true disciples will soon discover the cross of Christ. There they will see writ large the admonition of 1 Thessalonians 3:3 which advises us to be strengthened in our faith "so that no one would be disturbed by these afflictions; for you yourselves know that we have been destined for this." Even in what would seem to be the less arduous way, Jesus has not left us the slightest bit of room for the narcissistic materialism and love of ease that have tainted the modern doctrine of divine prosperity that is so often preached today. In contrast, the blessed and prosperous life that the apostles John and Paul describe in their epistles is an authentic, prosperous life in Christ only because it contains the cross and some measure of self-denial, long-suffering, and tribulation. This has always been and always will be the cost of His Kingdom and the portion of those who would be Christ's disciples.

The Land of Goshen

How can we explain divine prosperity to the modern Church? What would help us understand? I have found Israel's experience in the land of Goshen—their arrival, their permanence, and their departure for Canaan—to be a powerful illustration of what God considers prosperity to be.

Goshen was Israel's dwelling place from the lifetime of Joseph up until the Exodus. Goshen is the rich, fertile, delta land that lies at the mouth of and between the major branches of the Nile in Egypt. But how and when did Israel come to live in Goshen?

We know that God called Abraham and his family from Ur of the Chaldees to the land of Canaan about twenty centuries before Christ. God did not call Abraham as a poor man from a poor city to be an austere hermit, living a life of desert pilgrimage with an ass and a tent, but as a very rich man from a very rich empire to dwell in a new rich land. He was called from one earthly place to another earthly place, from the Fertile Crescent of Mesopotamia to Canaan land, a land that flowed with milk and honey. Canaan was a land of abundance. It was green, fertile, and covered with fields, vineyards and also dotted with prosperous little cities.

We must see that God called a rich man *from* and *to* a rich land. Of course, Canaan, though promised by God to Abraham, belonged to other men. The rich land of promise was just that—a promise. And the principal motive of Abraham's pilgrimage to and through Canaan was spiritual. He sought God, not riches or possessions. He already had great possessions.

We know that Abraham, Isaac, Jacob, and their descendants lived there for many generations as nomads. Though they wandered without houses or a city of their own, they were rich nomads living in a strange land with large valuable herds, silver, and gold. And though the blessing of God remained upon them as they moved about and pitched their tents in their adopted earthly paradise, they also suffered external trials, oppressions, and wars, along with internal strife and rivalries among their own brethren. The sons of Jacob, though blessed by God with prosperity, fought among themselves for paternal affection and for place and patrimony in their family. The prosperous life in Canaan included a full measure of bitterness and grief, as well as divine favor.

In the previous chapter, we mentioned how fraternal jealousy led Joseph's brothers to cast Jacob's favorite son into a pit and then sell him as a slave to the Ishmaelites to be carried into Egypt. When they returned home to their father, they told him that a wild beast had devoured their brother—a half-truth because, in a sense, the wild beast of satanic jealousy had indeed devoured Joseph. We can only imagine the anguish and grief in the heart of Jacob and his house. Rich and poor families alike suffer tragedies and tribulations. Ask a wealthy person, and he himself will tell you that though wealth may shield one from some of life's trials, wealth cannot completely protect the wealthy from the cup of suffering that all humanity must partake of from time to time. All of Jacob's natural prosperity was not able to return Joseph to his father.

Universal Poverty

During the time of Jacob and Joseph, there was a great drought and famine in all the Bible lands between the Nile and the Euphrates. What does universal drought and famine produce? Poverty, severe universal poverty. The Promised Land of Canaan, which once flowed with milk and honey, soon began to flow with dust and sand. Yet God had a plan to deliver His chosen people from the gross poverty that consumed Canaan, and that plan would be carried out through the life of Joseph. The abused and despised son who had been sold into slavery by his brothers was destined to become their deliverer. Despite long years of personal suffering, God would lift him out of his own poverty to show him favor and make him governor over all of Egypt.

During his tenure as Pharaoh's governor, he gathered and stored Egypt's harvests during seven years of plenty and then wisely administered and sold those stores of food during the seven years of drought and famine. Not only did Joseph preserve and enlarge Egypt and Pharaoh's wealth during a time of poverty, God enabled Joseph to deliver his own nation from poverty and even increased their wealth and well-being. The irony is that the prosperity of the House of Jacob was only made possible through Joseph's suffering and poverty. Where there is no cross, there cannot be divine prosperity.

After revealing himself to his brothers and to his father, Joseph and Pharaoh invited his family to live in Egypt. Pharaoh said to them, "The land of Egypt is at your disposal; settle your father and your brothers in the best of the land, let them live in the land of Goshen" (Gen. 47:6). Seventy souls—the entire nation of Israel—settled in the best land of Egypt and dwelt and prospered there for more than fifty years, during the lifetime of Joseph and the Pharaoh he served.

We arrived in Spain in 1983 as a young missionary couple. In those early days, Spain was poor—as well as the Teppers. We lived through and witnessed the next twenty-five years of Spain's miraculous transformation from poverty into one of the richest nations on the earth. Betel arrived in Russia during the first decade after the collapse of the former Soviet Union. In less than two decades, Russia was also transformed from a desperate, poverty-stricken nation into an economic superpower. Can we imagine the heights of prosperity Israel achieved during their favored, first half-century in Joseph's Egypt?

If Goshen was the best land in Egypt, why was it empty and offered to the sons of Jacob? Why did not the Egyptians themselves live there? We can only speculate. Goshen was a delta land inundated every year by the flooding of the

Nile. It was, therefore, a sparsely populated land. Egypt was a civilization that built fixed cities and lived in houses of brick and stone. They also built great stone temples and pyramids on such a grand scale that even after four millennia, modern man is still awed by their scope and size. That kind of civilization was not and could not be built in the delta lands of Lower Egypt, but rather on the higher bluffs along the banks of the Nile. The Egyptians, however, were content to allow laborers and slaves to sow the land of Goshen and to pastor their flocks there, but they themselves built no stone cities in Goshen. Only fools would build cities in a land which would regularly find itself under water—fools, Americans, and Dutchmen whose jetties and dykes give them at best tenuous protection from the seasonal flooding of their delta lands.

Pastors and nomads who lived in tents had no problem with the perennial inundations of the Nile. When the waters rose they simply picked up their homes and sought higher ground until the flood waters returned to their place. Goshen was a perfect fit for Israel's pilgrims. The consequences of living in Goshen, a rich and fertile though precarious land, were that Israel prospered under the patronage of Joseph and his Pharaoh. Their herds and harvests were multiplied each year. Under ideal conditions, agricultural productivity easily triumphs over craft and industrial productivity. Although this may seem like a quaint and ignorant statement to modern men infatuated with the miracles of modern science, technology, and the mass production of industrial goods, Matthew 13:8 tells us that a seed that fell into good ground and brought forth fruit "some a hundredfold, some sixty, and some thirty" would yield more each year than Microsoft or Google and is nothing short of a divine goldmine of prosperity. If a bull and cow or ram and ewe produce only one offspring each year, they are compounding at 50 percent their owner's wealth. Over 50 years, that will easily beat the best modern hedge fund's performance.

A Half-Century of Radical Prosperity

> But the sons of Israel were fruitful, and increased greatly, and multiplied, and became exceedingly mighty, so that the land was filled with them. (Exod. 1:7)

God willed that His people would prosper, and prosper they did, so much so that their numbers and wealth increased to the point that their power and presence posed a threat to their Egyptian overlords. After Joseph died and his fame and power faded into legend, "there arose up a new king over Egypt which knew not Joseph" (v. 8 KJV). Without Joseph, their patron and protector, and with a new Pharaoh who had no relationship to or sympathy for the House of Joseph, the existence of Israel became more precarious, and not simply because of the annual flooding of the land of Goshen, but because of Egypt's jealousy. It is curious how intertwined the blessing of divine prosperity and jealousy have been throughout the history of God's people.

Pharaoh viewed Israel's prosperity and enlargement as an existential threat to the Egyptian nation and said to his people,

> Behold, the people of the sons of Israel are more and mightier than we. Come, let us deal wisely with them, or else they will multiply and in the event of war, they will also join themselves to those who hate us, and fight against us and depart from the land. (Exod. 1:9-10)

The new Pharaoh then set taskmasters over Israel and enslaved them. They were forced to build his treasure cities of Pithom and Raamses. That Pharaoh and the Pharaohs who followed him enslaved Israel for four centuries, up until the time of Moses and the Exodus. In a very real sense, after the death of Joseph, Pharaoh's favor and the prosperity associated with his patronage first waned, and then lifted from the sons of Israel. Yet the favor of God and the blessing of His divine prosperity did not end with the world's disfavor. We read: "But the more they afflicted them, the more they multiplied and grew" (Exod. 1:12 KJV).

The Jews, God's chosen people, have always possessed a special gift: they know how to survive and prosper in the most difficult circumstances. They may be persecuted Russian peasants in the pogroms of the Czars, as portrayed in the popular musical *Fiddler On The Roof*. Though dangerously perched on the peak of the metaphorical roof of this world, they manage to scratch out a heartfelt tune on their fiddles without falling and breaking their necks. They may be poor German Jews like the Rothschild family, shut up in the narrow prison-like confines of the Frankfurt ghetto, yet still enabled by God to build the greatest family fortune of their age. The more the world abuses God's chosen, the more they prosper.

I believe Jews and Christians are called by God to live on the edge of a precarious pilgrimage, traveling between this world and eternity, in order that they may be blessed by His grace, despite all circumstances, despite all manner of human and demonic affliction. "But the more they afflicted them, the more they multiplied and grew." It is on that edge that true prosperity is found, and it is on that edge that God said to Abraham and his descendants, "And in you all families of the earth will be blessed" (Gen. 12:3).

In a little more than 400 years, Israel grew from seventy souls to a great nation of more than a million Israelites. Today, after more than 3,500 years of almost constant oppression, the Jews continue to be the most blessed, the most prosperous, and the most mistreated of all the peoples on the earth.

The Three Dimensions of Prosperity

Let us return to John's prayer: "Beloved, I pray that in all respects you may prosper and be in good health, just as your soul prospers." John's prayer touches the three dimensions of prosperity: the things that surround us, our bodies, and our souls. I believe that his definition lists the elements of the blessings of prosperity, but not in their order of importance. Those same three elements of prosperity are also mentioned in the book of Job, only in an inverse order.

Earlier, in chapter one, I described in detail the confrontation between the Lord and Satan where Satan attempted to provoke God against Job. Let us revisit that scene, and this time, look at it from another angle. In chapters one and two of the book of Job, we read that one day the sons of God came to present themselves before the

Lord. Satan somehow found his way into the courts of the Most High and presented himself before the Lord. When the Lord asked Satan where he had come from, He received a curt reply. Satan stated flatly that he had been patrolling up and down over all the earth, insinuating that he had been examining "his own" domain. The Lord reminded him that although Satan had indeed stolen the dominion over the earth from Adam, Adam and his seed had been subsequently redeemed by the Lord's own sacrifice, and that God still retained dominion over the redeemed of the human race. "Have you considered My servant Job? For there is no one like him on the earth, a blameless and upright man, fearing God, and turning away from evil." I note that the Lord was careful to emphasize that Job was His servant and not Satan's servant.

I can almost see the sneer on Satan's face as he challenged the Lord's appraisal of Job's character and motives. I read between the lines and hear Satan say, "Job does not serve You for nothing! You prosper him. Have You not set a hedge around his house and all his physical possessions on every side? Have You not blessed all that he has put his hand to do and made him a rich man with vast possessions? He does not serve You because he loves You. Touch what he has—take away his prosperity—and he will curse You to Your face."

The Lord's answer to Satan is very revealing. He accepted Satan's challenge. He essentially said, "You may touch one dimension of Job's prosperity. All his natural possessions are in your power, but do not touch Job himself." Of course, we know that within one single tragic hour, marauders stole all of Job's herds and wealth and killed his servants, and then a great whirlwind destroyed his eldest son's banqueting house, killing all of Job's sons and daughters.

When Job heard the devastating news, true to God's estimation of his character, he tore his clothing, shaved his head, fell to the ground, and worshiped God. He opened his mouth and cried out a stunning declaration of faith and loyalty that has strengthened and encouraged the Israel of God for almost four millennia:

> Naked came I out of my mother's womb,
> And naked I shall return there.
> The Lord gave and the Lord has taken away.
> Blessed be the name of the Lord. (Job 1:21)

God permitted the removal of the first and shallowest dimension of prosperity: the things that surrounded Job's life. I realize that I am oversimplifying, and I do not wish to imply that the lives of Job's children and servants are mere "things." They are not. What I am attempting to point out is that God allowed the stripping away of the tangible signs of prosperity that were external to Job himself.

In the second chapter of Job, we again see Satan presenting himself before the Lord in the courts of Heaven. The Lord confronted Satan and asked him if he had noticed that Job still held fast to his integrity "although you incited Me against him to ruin him without cause." Satan's reply is one of the most chilling quotes found in the Bible. In a single sarcastic reply, Satan purely distilled his cynicism, materialism, and defiance of evil: "Skin for skin! Yes, all that a man has he will give for his life. However, put forth Your hand now, and touch his bone and his flesh; he will curse You to Your face" (Job 2:3-5).

The Lord responded and said, "He is in your hand, but save his life. You may touch his health. You may strip away another layer of Job's prosperity, but do not touch his soul." We know that Satan proceeded to afflict Job with boils from the soles of his feet to the crown of his head, reducing the once healthy and rich Job to a poor man sitting in a heap of ashes, scratching himself with a broken potsherd.

As Job sat in his miserable state of suffering and loss, I believe Satan spoke through Job's wife, taunting him, "Do you still hold fast your integrity? Curse God and die!" (Job 2:9). Job turned to his wife and simply said, "What? Shall we receive good at the hand of God, and shall we not receive evil?" (Job 2:10 KJV). In all his misery and shame, Job accepted the portion God had permitted to be measured to him and did not sin with his lips.

It is very important for us to see that God did not afflict Job. God is never the author of evil, but rather He permitted Satan to afflict His servant Job. Some translations of Job 2:10 read, "Shall we indeed accept good from God and not accept adversity?" God permitted adversity in Job's life, not evil. But why would a good and loving God even permit the righteous to suffer? Why would an all-powerful God permit a lesser creature like Satan to hurt one of His favorite servants? What possible purpose could God have in Job's affliction? Alexander Solzhenitsyn, the great modern Russian author and Nobel laureate, who endured suffering and persecution in the prison camps of the Soviet Gulag could say, "The meaning of earthly existence lies not, as we have grown used to thinking, in prospering, but in the development of the soul." Perhaps God was more concerned with the development of Job's soul than in his mere natural prosperity and temporal happiness? Perhaps He permitted Satan to afflict His beloved servant so that a far greater and eternal good might be wrought within Job's soul.

Is not the whole purpose of life the progress of the soul towards God? The only end that events, blessings, afflictions, abundance, want, favor, or rejection have—whether we deem them good or bad—is the progress of the soul towards God.

Prosperity, then, is all that helps us in our pilgrimage towards God, and the end of prosperity is to be conformed to His image. We are prospered, whether it be by the favor of a Pharaoh who knows and loves Joseph, or by the ill will of a Pharaoh who knows not Joseph and hates the Israel of God. By faith and trust "we know that God causes all things to work together for good to those who love God, to those who are called according to His purpose" (Rom. 8:28).

The Safest Most Prosperous Place

'You yourselves have seen what I did to the Egyptians, and how I bore you on eagles' wings, and brought you to Myself.' (Exod. 19:4)

I believe the secret of prosperity is found in one Person and one place: In God and in Goshen. Goshen is more than the delta lands of Egypt. It is that special place God has ordained for those He loves. In reality, it can be any place, if we have discovered that "in him we live, and move, and have our being" (Acts 17:28 KJV). Those who are tough, humble and broken often find it first, and those who have discovered how to abide in God and their Goshen in good times and bad times will always enjoy divine prosperity. It is the safest place in the universe for those who love God.

The real danger lies in seeking prosperity someplace else other than God and the Goshen He has ordained for us. Pharaoh resisted the will of God and refused to let the people of Israel go to worship the Lord their God. His rebellion caused God to send ten terrible plagues over the land of Egypt. Pharaoh's Egypt suffered greatly, but the Israel of God was untouched by the plagues because they abided in Him and in the Goshen He chose for them. It is better to be a slave and poor in Goshen, than to be rich and dwell in the cities of Egypt when hail falls like stones, and darkness covers the earth.

While the first nine plagues did not touch the land of Goshen, the tenth plague, the Angel of Death, did visit Goshen, but not all of Goshen. There was a very special place even within the land of Goshen. On Israel's last night in Egypt, God instructed His people to gather house by house to eat the Passover together. They were told to sacrifice a lamb without blemish for their house:

> Moreover, they shall take some of the blood and put it on the two doorposts and on the lintel of the houses in which they eat it … Now you shall eat it in this manner: with

your loins girded, your sandals on your feet, and your staff in your hand; and you shall eat it in haste—it is the Lord's Passover. For I will go through the land of Egypt on that night, and will strike down all the firstborn in the land of Egypt, both man and beast; and against all the gods of Egypt I will execute judgments—I am the Lord. The blood shall be a sign for you on the houses where you live; and when I see the blood I will pass over you, and no plague will befall you to destroy you when I strike the land of Egypt. (Exod. 12:7-13)

If all the world is dying, and you and your house are saved, what is that called? Divine prosperity.

6

They Had Everything Except the One Thing They Lacked

In an earlier chapter, I asked the question, "What is prosperity? Is it good? Is it bad? Is it the will of God?" My simple answer was, "Yes, it is good, and it is the will of God—if it is well seasoned by the cross, and if the people of God never lose sight of the principal purpose of the Christian life which is the progress of the soul towards God.

When I pray for my family and for my friends, I ask God to prosper them. But I condition my prayer with Proverbs 10:22 "The blessing of the Lord, it maketh rich, and he addeth no sorrow with it" (KJV). I ask God to enlarge them and bless them, and indeed to prosper them, but to add no sorrow. It is true. Riches can bring happiness, but they can also bring sorrow. When Moses neared the end of his life, the Lord instructed him to warn Israel concerning the dangers they would face after his death, not from external enemies or plagues or natural disasters, but from the blessings, riches, and prosperity that would accrue to them as they fully inherited and possessed the land of Canaan:

> "Now therefore, write this song for yourselves, and teach it to the sons of Israel; put it on their lips … For when I bring them into the land flowing with milk and honey, which I swore to their fathers, and they have eaten and are satisfied and become prosperous, then they will turn to other gods and serve them, and spurn Me and break My covenant." (Deut. 31:19-20)

Israel and the Church have often been spoiled by the blessings of God. When they were lean and hungry, they offered thanksgiving for their daily bread, but once they enjoyed a season of prosperity, they habitually forgot who was responsible for their prosperity. Too often, the people of God have overindulged on the good things given to them, only to turn and worship the gifts of prosperity more than the Giver of prosperity. Prosperity, as wonderful as it is, has a downside. It can be dangerous and suffocating, and it may lead to idolatry and personal destruction. It is good, then, to temper our request for blessings from the Lord with this petition:

> Give me neither poverty nor riches;
> Feed me with the food that is my portion,
> That I not be full and deny You and say, "Who is the Lord?"
> Or that I not be in want and steal,
> And profane the name of my God. (Prov. 30:8-9)

To have everything in abundance is no guarantee of happiness, but then neither is living in poverty. The right balance is struck when we are content with what we have and with what we do not have.

Riches and Happiness

Let us consider the life and story of a rich family—a very rich, pious, and noble family in the Bible. They possessed everything, except the one thing they lacked to truly make them happy. The first book of Samuel begins with the story of a certain man by the name of Elkanah and his two wives: Hannah and Peninnah.

Elkanah and his wives lived in Ramathaim-zophim, which in Hebrew means "the high field of the watchman" or "a high and exalted place." Metaphorically and in actuality, they lived on top of the world. They were a wealthy family whose estate was situated on the highest and most secure site in the hill country of Ephraim. From their home, they enjoyed the best view of their lands and possessions. Elkanah's first wife, Hannah, was sterile but much loved by her husband. Her name in Hebrew meant "full of grace." His second wife, Peninnah or "pearl," was young, beautiful, and fertile. She was the mother of at least four children. As with most polygamous families, there was the inevitable strife and competition between the wives for the affection of their common husband. The younger, fruitful wife mocked and provoked the older, beloved wife because she was sterile and childless. The younger wife also envied the older, because she was more loved and each year received a double portion from Elkanah when the family went up to Shiloh to sacrifice before the Lord. On the other hand, Hannah, the older wife, envied the younger because she gave Elkanah children, while she remained childless. Elkanah dearly loved Hannah and comforted her, saying, "Why do you weep and why do you not eat and why is your heart sad? Am I not better to you than ten sons?" (1 Sam. 1:8). Yet Hannah, having everything: wealth and a devoted, loving husband, was sad. Though she lived in a "high and exalted place," she possessed everything except the one thing she lacked—the one thing that would make her happy—a son.

Hannah was a godly woman who prayed continually. One day she made a vow and said, "O Lord of hosts, if You will indeed look on the affliction of Your maidservant and remember me, and not forget Your maidservant, but will give Your maidservant a son, then I will give him to the Lord all the days of his life" (1 Sam. 1:11). Consider the irony of her vow. The one thing she lacked, the one thing that would complete her happiness, she asked of the Lord with the promise of once possessing it, to give it back to the Lord forever.

As she wept and prayed before the Lord at Shiloh, Eli, the high priest, observed her praying and mistook her grief for drunkenness. He reproved her as if she were a worthless, wicked woman of Belial. But she protested and revealed her heart and petition to the high priest. Eli immediately discerned the sincerity of her heart and said, "Go in peace, and may the God of Israel grant your petition that you have asked of Him" (1 Sam. 1:17).

Hannah returned home to Elkanah, and in the course of time, God gave her a son. She named him Samuel, which in Hebrew means, "asked of God." Hannah received just what she asked for and then, after three years, she kept her vow and offered Samuel to the Lord, placing him in the service of Eli at the tabernacle in Shiloh. Apparently, there was something she loved even more than her own happiness.

The Lord Makes Poor and Rich; He Brings Low, He Also Exalts

After Hannah kept her vow, she sang a song of thanksgiving:

> My heart exults in the Lord;
> My horn is exalted in the Lord,
> My mouth speaks boldly against my enemies,
> Because I rejoice in Your salvation.
>
> There is no one holy like the Lord,
> Indeed, there is no one besides You,
> Nor is there any rock like our God.
>
> Boast no more so very proudly,
> Do not let arrogance come out of your mouth;
> For the Lord is a God of knowledge,
> And with Him actions are weighed.
>
> The bows of the mighty are shattered,
> But the feeble gird on strength.
>
> Those who were full hire themselves out for bread,
> But those who were hungry cease to hunger.
> Even the barren gives birth to seven,
> But she who has many children languishes.

The Lord kills and makes alive;
He brings down to Sheol and raises up.

The Lord makes poor and rich;
He brings low, He also exalts.

He raises the poor from the dust,
He lifts the needy from the ash heap
To make them sit with nobles,
And inherit a seat of honor;
For the pillars of the earth are the Lord's,
And He set the world on them.
He keeps the feet of His godly ones,
But the wicked ones are silenced in darkness;
For not by might shall a man prevail.

Those who contend with the Lord will be shattered;
Against them He will thunder in the heavens,
The Lord will judge the ends of the earth;
And He will give strength to His king,
And will exalt the horn of His anointed. (1 Sam. 2:1-10)

I have always loved Hannah's song. Not only does she affirm that the "first will be last and the last will be first," but in her prophetic vision, she lifts us up to a new, heroic, celestial dimension. Her struggle with sterility, humiliation, shame and an arrogant human rival is elevated to a fight against universal enemies on the earth and in the Heavens. Her personal battle is transformed into warfare against the hosts of evil and death itself. In 1 Samuel 2:6, Scripture tells us that "the Lord kills and makes alive; He brings down to Sheol and raises up." He is the Lord of the resurrection. If the Most High God is the Lord of Heaven and of earth and has all power over all the enemies of life and over death itself, then it is a small thing for the God of the resurrection to make us rich and happy.

Hannah discovered the secret to true riches and divine prosperity. She had almost everything, but lacked the one thing that would make her happy. What did she do? She asked God for it, promising to place it upon the altar of sacrifice. By giving up the desire of her heart, did she fail to attain the son and the joy that she sought? No. She obtained all and more. She received a miraculous son. She received joy unspeakable and even a prophetic vision of the resurrection, and with her vision, a foretaste of the powers of the age to come. Once she honored her vow and returned Samuel to the Lord, she also received many more sons and daughters.

But how can it be that we prosper, renouncing what we esteem to be the missing piece in the puzzle we conceive to be our prosperity? It is because we only gain all when we sacrifice all, which is nothing less and nothing more than the cost of the Kingdom.

> "He who loves father or mother more than Me is not worthy of Me; and he who loves son or daughter more than Me is not worthy of Me. And he who does not take his cross and follow after Me is not worthy of Me. He who has found his life will lose it, and he who has lost his life for My sake will find it." (Matt. 10:37-39)

The one thing that everyone lacks which will make his happiness complete is the possession of "Christ in us" as our hope of glory. Our life and the things we are asked to place upon the altar are nothing—small dust in the balance—when compared to the life in Christ we gain. Jim Elliot, a young American missionary in Ecuador, put it this way shortly before he was martyred by the Auca Indians, "He is no fool who gives what he cannot keep to gain that which he cannot lose."

Mystery Abused

The sincerity of humble Christians who would please God by sacrificing all has often been mocked and abused by cynical men. H. L. Mencken, a skeptic and critic of Christianity, often mocked the naivety and gullibility of Christians. He once defined a demagogue as "one who preaches doctrines he knows to be untrue to men he knows to be idiots." Sometimes, it almost seems to me that H. L. Mencken's cynical and searing definition of the demagogue who appeals to and manipulates his listeners´ desires and prejudices is an apt description of modern prosperity preachers and their flocks. Those preachers twist the biblical mysteries of sacrifice and consecration to abuse and make merchandise of the people who sincerely want to place their all upon the altar. The duped give them their money, their cars, and even their homes in hope of pleasing God. Many of the faithful who respond to the modern prosperity message sincerely and altruistically want to give unto God. Some only offer unto God with the hope that they may receive the added perk of material riches.

God, however, is God and no demagogue. Our motives and the preacher's motives may be mixed, but His motives are pure. He already owns all the cattle on a thousand hills and the universe besides. He needs nothing from man and, unlike the modern prosperity preacher, when He asks for sacrifice from us, it is to ultimately enrich us and not Himself.

All who truly desire divine prosperity must, like Hannah, allow God to define and mete out their portion. He has the power to make us rich or poor and the power to bring us down or raise us up. Jesus asks no more from us than the Father asked of Him. Jesus made Himself poor that we might become rich, and in the process He was ultimately exalted to become King of Kings and Lord of Lords, to sit on the right hand of God the Father. This is the path revealed in Hannah's song that leads to true divine prosperity: "He raiseth up the poor out of the dust, and lifteth up the beggar from the dunghill, to set them among princes, and to make them inherit the throne of glory" (1 Sam. 2:8 KJV).

In the twentieth century, Dr. Viktor Frankl, a survivor of Nazi concentration camps, in his preface to *Man's Search For Meaning*, identified this same mystery in the heart of those inmates who found nobility and meaning in their suffering. What was their secret? Man discovers true happiness only through the surrender of one's self and destiny to something higher than self:

> For success, like happiness, cannot be pursued; it must ensue, and it only does so as the unintended side-effect of one's personal dedication to a cause greater than oneself or as the by-product of one's surrender to a person other than oneself. Happiness must happen … You have to let it happen by not caring about it … Then you will live to see that in the long run—in the long run, I say! Success will follow you precisely because you had forgotten to think of it.

If Jesus trod that path to glory, then we must tread the same path. The poor will be raised from the dust just as the first Adam must be raised from the earthly and changed into the heavenly, to be transformed into the image of the second Adam who is Christ. Perhaps the beggar may be changed into a prince or a philanthropist in this life. Perhaps he may have to wait and remain in humble circumstances before he is lifted up in eternity. But those who place all upon the altar and who leave the Lord to define and mete out their portion can be sure that one day they will be "set among princes" and will, in eternity's day, "inherit thrones of glory."

Therefore, our perspective ought to be that the end of divine prosperity is the progress of our soul towards God, and grasping that, we will also come to understand that God's purpose for us is that we might more than merely prosper in this present life. He seeks much more: that we might eternally prosper and inherit a place of honor. Whatever God puts in our hands while we walk upon the earth, whatever He withholds from our hands while time exists, whatever we are able to place upon His altar, only has meaning as it contributes to His ultimate goal: that we might inherit a throne of glory at His side. There we will find true divine prosperity where it has always been hidden from the natural man's eyes: in the mystery of the cross of Christ, just where Ahmet the plumber told us it would be found. We will discover that "now we have something much better than what we lost."

Behold, I Thought ... But Now I Know

Would that we all were as good and brave and sacrificial as Hannah the Ephraimite and Ahmet the plumber. But most of us are not. Neither are we willing to let God mete out our portion. And though we know what we should do and where the path to true happiness and prosperity lies, it is hard for us to walk that way, and harder still to place our all upon His altar.

There was another man who had everything but the one thing that would make him happy. Like Elkanah and Hannah, he also was very rich and powerful. Nevertheless, happiness eluded him. I am thinking of Naaman the Syrian. We find his story in the second book of Kings: "Now Naaman, captain of the host of the king of Syria, was a great man with his master, and honorable, because by him the Lord had given deliverance unto Syria: he was also a mighty man in valor, but he was a leper" (2 Kings 5:1 KJV).

The world is full of great and powerful men—men who have fought and clawed their way to the top of the pile and then stood and stomped upon the faces of their peers as they struggled to climb the greased pole to the pinnacle of power. But Naaman was not like other great men. He must have been an extraordinary human being, especially when one considers the pagan cultural milieu in which he lived. For not only was he a great and powerful man, but he was an honorable man and a deliverer who, through his valor and skill, saved his nation in time of war. He was a hero whose life was made of the stuff bards and storytellers turn into songs and local legends.

His story might have stopped right there in his own nation in the ninth century before Christ or perhaps lingered for a few generations more in the tales and songs of his people.

But it did not. Today, almost thirty centuries later, his name and his story are still remembered by countless Jews and Christians over the whole earth. Why? Because he was a great and mighty man of valor? No. But because he was a leper who found healing and, through his healing, faith in the God of Israel. It is strange, but wonderful. Sometimes it is not strength and personal glory that make men great, but their weaknesses and their struggles, and their final triumph over those very weaknesses. What seems to blight our lives may actually turn out to be what finally sets us on high.

Can we imagine the inner struggle in Naaman's heart? He could not help but to have asked what lasting value lay in his beauty, wealth, power, and the esteem of his king and nation, when his own body began to rot and decay before his eyes. Surely Naaman knew that his favor and fame would soon fade and be overtaken by ostracism, revulsion, and finally death. He knew that if he were to be remembered at all, his story would be tragic. That one thing that he lacked was like a fly in his ointment. It robbed all of his most precious possessions of their value. Though Naaman might have enjoyed the glow of his nation's adulation, and though he commanded the army of his king, and though he dwelt in the spacious luxury of a mansion with slaves and servants, he must have felt poor and miserable as he sat and meditated upon his rotting skin wrapped in bandages.

How was Naaman lifted on high? How did he recover his health? We know from the account of Naaman's life in the second book of Kings that the Syrians had raided Israel and taken captive a very young girl, a little maid, and sold her into slavery. She had become the servant of Naaman's wife. In the ancient world there was often much ill will between slaves and their masters. The first generation of slaves who had been captured in warfare inevitably remembered the slaughter of their loved ones and the defeat of their nation with bitterness. More often than not, they despised their new masters and were forced to serve through fear and compulsion. Rarely was there affection and love between master and servant.

But in Naaman's house, one reads between the lines and senses affection and intimacy in the relationship between the little maid and her mistress, and a heartfelt concern on the part of the maid for the health and well-being of Naaman, her master. She said to her mistress, "I wish that my master were with the prophet who is in Samaria! Then he would cure him of his leprosy" (2 Kings 5:3). I hear in the voice of that young girl the kind of love—agape love—that is only found in the living faith of someone who knows the God of Israel. What is equally remarkable is the reaction of Naaman's wife and of Naaman himself. She humbled herself and listened, and believed the word of the little maid. Then she went straight to her husband and conveyed the maid's claim to him. He too believed and went right to his king and told him what the Jewish slave had told him. The king of Syria responded without hesitation and said, "Go now, and I will send a letter to the king of Israel" (2 Kings 5:5). Think of the greatness of this man Naaman. What kind of man could command and simultaneously capture the affection of his slave and his king? Only a very good and noble man, someone who was loyal to his own master and kind to his own slaves.

Naaman gathered together gifts for the prophet, a fortune: ten talents of silver, six thousand pieces of gold, and ten changes of raiment. Just the gold alone would be worth approximately one million dollars in real terms today. Sometimes what we do not have is worth more than all we have. Naaman acted like Shakespeare's Richard III whose desperate cry, "A horse! a horse! my kingdom for a horse!" has been the cry of many men and women throughout the ages. Naaman's lavish gift is then not so striking, but that which men do when they have everything but the one thing that will make them happy. Naaman desperately wanted to be healed.

When Naaman presented the king of Syria's letter with his petition to the king of Israel, the king of Israel was greatly distressed and tore his clothes, crying out, "Am I God, to kill and to make alive?" He feared that the king of Syria was seeking a pretext to quarrel with him—to draw Israel into war. But when Elisha the prophet heard of the king's distress, he sent him word, "Why have you torn your clothes? Now let him come to me, and he shall know that there is a prophet in Israel" (2 Kings 5:7-8).

The king of Israel then communicated Elisha's instructions to Naaman, and Naaman and his company went with his horses and chariot and stood in front of Elisha's house. I can see a great cloud of dust rising up behind Naaman and his servants with their horses loaded with gifts, silver, and gold as they approached Elisha's home. I can see Naaman standing expectantly in his chariot alongside his driver, waiting for the famous prophet of Israel to step outside his home to greet him and to receive him with the respect and protocol Naaman's station deserved. But it did not happen that way. The Scripture says:

> Elisha sent a messenger to him, saying, "Go and wash in the Jordan seven times, and your flesh will be restored to you and you will be clean." But Naaman was furious and went away and said, "Behold, I thought, 'He will surely come out to me and stand and call on the name of the Lord his God, and wave his hand over the place and cure the leper.' Are not Abanah and Pharpar, the rivers of Damascus, better than all the waters of Israel? Could I not wash in them and be clean?" So he turned and went away in a rage. (2 Kings 5:10-12)

Why would such a good man like Naaman react the way he did? If he was willing to take the word of a slave girl and travel to a far country, to a country his own nation had often warred with, and offer a fortune to be healed, why did he go into a rage and refuse to obey the simple command of the prophet? Surely, that act of obedience was small change in the balance compared to all Naaman had already willingly offered for his healing.

Perhaps it is because there is a gatekeeper—Adamic pride—who guards that one thing we lack. Pride has denied the rich and the poor, the weak and the powerful access to the divine prosperity and blessing God has intended for their lives. It is that one simple, unimportant thing we cannot yield to God that often causes us to stumble. Naaman may have been a noble and good man as far as men esteem goodness, but he, like all men, was a son of Adam. When God chooses to bless, He knows exactly what to ask us for in return—total surrender, that one last valueless trinket Adam is reluctant to place, but must place, upon the altar.

Naaman went away in a rage. He wanted a better plan. We may acknowledge that the God of Israel is the Great Physician and go to Him promising much for His help, but when He recommends the removal of what we regard as precious, we often seek a second opinion from other sources of deliverance and healing, hoping for less stringent terms.

Naaman's servant turned to his master and said, "My father, had the prophet told you to do some great thing, would you not have done it?" (2 Kings 5:13). This was not a safe move on the servant's part. When a great, powerful, pagan general is in a rage, why would a servant dare to challenge his judgment and cross his will, thus exposing himself to his master's wrath? I would venture that in most cases he would be risking a severe reprimand or a physical blow, or worse. A slave in that culture and age was a mere chattel and could be punished, beaten, sold, or killed as his master saw fit. Could it be that the servant, like the little maid, loved his master and knew his heart? I wonder how many servants in the ancient Middle East called their masters "my father"? The servant knew his master well. Naaman heeded his counsel and obeyed the prophet's command. He washed himself seven times in the River Jordan and was healed.

Hannah, after years of humiliation, was willing to put upon the altar the one thing she lacked and had asked the Lord for—a son. She was given true happiness and blessing beyond her dreams in return. Naaman, after receiving a single, sudden, unexpected command that crossed his will, humbled himself and was finally willing to put upon the altar the one thing he did not wish to part with—his wounded pride, that he might receive what he lacked—healing and faith in the Living God. How much better it is to let God choose for us. He has told us,

"For My thoughts are not your thoughts,
Nor are your ways My ways," declares the Lord.

"For as the heavens are higher than the earth,
So are My ways higher than your ways and My thoughts than your thoughts." (Isa. 55:8-9)

7

They Had Nothing Left to Give
Save Ashes

In 1930, C. T. Studd was drawing near the end of his life in the Congo, in the heart of Africa. He received a visit from his daughter. On their last day together, knowing that they would never see each other again in this world, he wanted to give her a gift, something significant with which to remember him. He searched around his large, straw-walled and thatched-roof dwelling for an heirloom, for something sentimental. After a few moments he turned to her and said, "I have nothing to give you. I have given everything away a long time ago." This is quite a statement from the son of a millionaire who gave his large inheritance away in a single day four decades earlier, as a young missionary in inland China. The simplicity of the setting of this anecdote and the tenderness in the father's acknowledgment that he had nothing left to give his daughter goes right to the heart of the cost of the Kingdom of God.

C. T. Studd had given God his heart and all his earthly wealth a long time ago, and in so doing, he had given his daughter, the Church, and the world the example of his life. What more can be asked of any man or woman?

Over the last forty years, we have discovered as missionaries that the best place to find costly sacrifice and true prosperity is in the heart of people who have nothing left to give. C. T. Studd came from a very wealthy and famous family. When God asked him for all, he gave it without hesitation. We have worked during most of our ministry years among the poor and marginalized—among addicts, alcoholics, unemployed immigrants, and the homeless. Like C. T. Studd, when they arrive in our Betel communities, they have nothing left to give, not because they have given all in heroic sacrifice in obedience to the King of Heaven, but because they have often squandered their lives on sin and debauchery, leaving nothing for themselves, their families, or God. In one sense, there is quite a difference between C. T. Studd and the outcasts who enter Betel. In another sense, at the end of the day, C. T. Studd, the *Betelitos*, and all men stand on the same ground.

I can remember being invited to testify one Wednesday evening in 1973 in the chapel at Temple Baptist Church in Wilmington, North Carolina. I was a very young Christian, and this was the first time I had been invited to speak in the church where Mary had grown up. I am not exaggerating when I say that our marriage was a bit incomprehensible to the godly folk at Temple Baptist. Mary had grown up in

Temple's Sunday school, been saved and baptized at nine years of age there, and as an adult was held in esteem as a highly qualified and professional public school counselor. She had been a faithful member of the Temple congregation all her life and was respected for her good judgment—that is, until she met and married me. I was a recently converted northern Jew who had followed my mother south shortly after my conversion. I had come from an unusual background. On one hand, I, too, was from a highly qualified professional background: Lehigh, Cambridge, and Harvard universities, and an executive position as the assistant to the treasurer of the Boston Museum of Fine Arts. But on the other hand, I had taken a detour through the counterculture while at Harvard and the Boston Museum of Fine Arts. During that time, I had lived for three years in a commune and all that implied concerning drugs, immorality, and lifestyle. When I arrived in Wilmington shortly after my conversion, I had long hair, wore "holy" (as in full of holes) dungarees, and had taken Mary away from Temple Baptist to a small Pentecostal church. For a conservative Southern Baptist congregation, a converted, northern, Jewish hippy of Pentecostal-Charismatic persuasion was a different kind of Christian than they were accustomed to. Novel, yes, but also dubious.

I gave my testimony and drew a parallel of my life before and after Christ to that of the Apostle Paul's life. I read from Philippians:

> But whatever things were gain to me, those things I have counted as loss for the sake of Christ. More than that, I count all things to be loss in view of the surpassing

> value of knowing Christ Jesus my Lord, for whom I have suffered the loss of all things, and count them but rubbish so that I may gain Christ, and may be found in Him, not having a righteousness of my own derived from the Law, but that which is through faith in Christ, the righteousness which comes from God on the basis of faith, that I may know Him and the power of His resurrection and the fellowship of His sufferings, being conformed to His death; in order that I may attain to the resurrection from the dead. (Phil. 3:7-11)

I thought that the parallel was reasonable. Paul and I were both Jews. We both had backgrounds and accomplishments in education, culture, and society that we had turned our backs upon to follow Christ. I thought I felt, at least in some degree, Paul's passion to know the power of Christ's resurrection. However, I was surprised to discover that not everyone thought my comparison was valid. After the meeting as we were leaving, the pastor came up to me and rebuked me. He was an intern pastor who had recently replaced Pastor Parkerson, the pastor who had married us at Temple Baptist. The intern pastor did not know me personally; in fact, it was the first time we had met, and his rebuke was rather sharp. He said, "You have some nerve comparing yourself to the Apostle Paul. He was a godly man who lived a perfect life before the Law. He was a religious leader in his nation, perhaps even the future High Priest of the Jews. You were a sinful, immoral drug addict. While I am glad that you have gotten saved, I do not see how your life was at all like the life of Paul."

I was taken aback. My first thought was, "He is right. I am a proud and presumptuous fool for even suggesting that my experience was like Paul's." True, Paul was certainly wrong in his self-righteousness and in his persecution of the Church, but he had been a moral man trying to please God through obedience to the Law. I also was a sinner, but I had not been a good or moral man. I never even tried to be righteous like Paul the Pharisee, but assumed God accepted my poor excuse for good behavior as righteousness. It was true—everything he said. I had no sense of sin, even when I sinned before I knew Christ. I felt like an idiot as I stumbled around and tried to explain to the rather imposing, scholarly Baptist pastor that I had only wanted to say that Paul and I were Jews who lost everything to follow Christ, and of course I knew what I had lost was little in comparison to Paul's loss. The pastor was not impressed.

Later, as I thought about his criticism, I could see that perhaps he had been a bit too hard on me. In my testimony, I had also quoted Philippians 3:12, "Not that I have already obtained it or have already become perfect, but I press on so that I may lay hold of that for which also I was laid hold of by Christ Jesus." I had not claimed to have been or to be perfect, just to have left behind what I was and what I possessed to follow after and obtain Christ. The more I thought about his criticism, the more I realized God would have to sort out that rebuke, not me. At the time I remembered having read somewhere in the Bible, "Let a righteous man reprove you. It shall be as a pleasant oil." But the pastor's oil did not feel too pleasant to me. In fact, it burned and I felt rather foolish and humbled.

Some Things Grow Best in Ashes

During our early years as missionaries in Mexico, we spent most of our time working among the university students at the *Universidad de las Américas*—an elite and largely privileged group of men and woman. In the last three decades we have labored mostly, though not exclusively, with humbler folk—the marginalized of society who have made a muck of their lives. Over the years, we have seen tens of thousands find Christ in the Betel communities and churches around the world. We have also seen God's hand upon many men and woman who have responded to His call and left all to follow Christ in heroic sacrifice. To be honest, their sacrifices have been a bit more like mine than Paul's or C. T. Studd's. We have had nothing to leave behind, nothing to offer up of value, save our dissolute and broken lives. Some *Betelitos* have gone on to live extraordinary lives and have brought great glory to God and have enlarged His Kingdom. A few have attained to true greatness in God. Watching them over the years, I am persuaded that the ashes of broken and bankrupt lives are the best soil in which to sow the seed of Christ's Kingdom. Why?

Very early on, we tell our people that they are called and destined for greatness in God, and if they will seek first the Kingdom of God and His righteousness, at whatever the cost, they will eventually find that the will of God for their lives is, indeed, true divine prosperity. For most, at first, this is an outrageous and unsubstantial claim—a fantasy. They look at their circumstances and all they have lost in life: their families, their health, their material possessions, their confidence—absolutely everything, and they stand bewildered. Rather than helping them, we have confused them. They know in their hearts that the divine prosperity we are putting before them must be a fairy tale beyond their reach. Before they start their journey in God, they stand bewildered and empty-handed, desiring to offer something of value, but with nothing to offer. But that very sense of impotence and bankruptcy is exactly the self-recognition God seeks in all He would make rich.

I remember one Sunday we asked Ramon, a young man who had entered our community many years earlier as a drug addict, to give his testimony in the Madrid church. He climbed the steps to the platform, stood before the microphone, and said in a soft voice, "When I came to Betel I had nothing. Now I have everything. I have Christ, a wife, a child, a ministry and my life back." He went on in more detail, but what he said I have heard hundreds of times before. And every time I hear a new permutation of that same story, my heart leaps for joy, knowing that God gives beauty for ashes.

Ramon found everything when he found God. I believe he discovered true divine prosperity, not the modern version of prosperity whose message sounds like a clanging cymbal to men and woman who sit in the ashes and remains of their broken lives.

Ziklag

In an earlier chapter we examined David's desperate cry to God for help in the eighteenth Psalm, when Saul and his army had surrounded and trapped David and his men on a great rock in the wilderness. We noted that God heard his cry and comforted him. David was lifted up and set in a broad place of fellowship and revelation, and then delivered for a season from Saul's wrath, but only for a season. David's story, though punctuated with blessings and deliverances, still had a long way to go before its final happy ending. In fact, God intended to bring David to the edge of doom. He would sow His Kingdom in the ashes of David's life by allowing him to pass through even deeper personal tragedy. This was the cost David was called to pay for the Kingdom and a messianic line of kings.

David was the eighth son of Jesse. He was the least of all the sons. We all know his story: how David was held back by his father while his older brothers went to war with Saul against the Philistines, of David being sent to his brothers with provisions, and of his providential victory over Goliath, and then of his promotion in Saul's court, his friendship with Jonathan, and his marriage to Saul's daughter Michal. We know that David grew in fame and stature in the eyes of the Jewish nation. They sang his praise, "Saul has slain his thousands, and David his ten thousands." We remember Saul's jealousy and repeated attacks against David and then David fleeing into the wilderness to save his life.

The Scriptures tell us that the discontented, the bitter in soul, the distressed, and the debtors followed David into the hills of Judah. We read of David's long years of wandering in the wilderness as a fugitive, pursued by Saul and his army, and finally being forced to take refuge in the land of the Philistines. David and his men had become a band of outcasts without a nation. David soon won the heart of Achish, the king of the Philistines and was given a place in his court and the village of Ziklag for his followers. Though Achish desired to show him favor, his captains distrusted David and his Hebrew refugees. When the Philistines and Israel were about to enter into open war, David was obligated to accompany his new lord and the Philistine army into battle against his own people. In his heart, David had remained a lover of God and the nation of Israel. This was indeed a bitter dilemma. Had his life come to this? The anointed and beloved hero of Israel seemed trapped by circumstances without any honorable way forward. Providentially, the Philistine lords refused to allow David and his men to go with them into battle, and Achish reluctantly dismissed them. They separated themselves from the Philistine army and returned to their families and the possessions they had left behind in the village of Ziklag. The Scriptures read:

Then it happened when David and his men came to Ziklag on the third day, that the Amalekites had made a raid on the Negev and on Ziklag, and had overthrown Ziklag and burned it with fire; and they took captive the women and all who were in it, both small and great, without killing anyone, and carried them off and went their way. When David and his men came to the city, behold, it was burned with fire, and their wives and their sons and their daughters had been taken captive. Then David and the people who were with him lifted their voices and wept until there was no strength in them to weep. Now David's two wives had been taken captive, Ahinoam the Jezreelitess and Abigail the widow of Nabal the Carmelite. Moreover David was greatly distressed because the people spoke of stoning

him, for all the people were embittered, each one because
of his sons and his daughters. But David strengthened
himself in the Lord his God. (1 Sam. 30:1-6)

Can we imagine a greater personal tragedy and disaster
than the one David and his men encountered when they
returned to their homes? All was destroyed. They sat
down in ashes and wept until they had no more tears to
weep. They had lost their wives, children, homes, herds,
and possessions. Though Ziklag was a poor excuse for
a home, it was the only home David and his band of
refugees possessed. As they wept in the smoke and the
charred ruins of Ziklag, the men began to murmur. They
had followed David in hope of finding a place in the
world. His initial glories and charisma had inspired them
to dream of the restoration of all they had lost in Saul's
kingdom. But now, suddenly, what little that remained of
their lives as refugees and fugitives was dashed into what
seemed to be an unredeemable wreckage and ruin. Who
was to blame? David had promised them a new life at his
side, but had utterly failed them. Some of the men talked
of stoning their captain. This was irrational, but despair
and grief can be as cruel as they are hopeless.

I can imagine what David must have thought when all
hope was gone and his own life was about to come to an
end at the hands of his own men, men he loved. David must
have felt the loss of his wives and children and possessions
as keenly as his men. But added onto this, David had to bear
the stinging rejection of his men, the latest in the long line
of rejections that followed David throughout his life. Had
he not been marginalized by his family as the youngest son,

perhaps even the son of a concubine and not Jesse's legitimate wife? Had he not served Saul faithfully and honored and protected his king's life, only to be pursued almost to death by Saul and his army? Achish and his captains had rejected him. And now his own men who once rallied around him and sang his praises talked of stoning him.

What did David do? Like all men of flesh and bones, he wept. But David was not entirely like all men. Though he was an ordinary man, he was a man called by God to greatness. Out of his distress, as he sat in ashes, David's heart rose up. He lifted his eyes to Heaven. And there, from that inner, higher place, the Scriptures tell us that "David encouraged himself in the Lord."

As all collapsed around David and his men, David was still the young shepherd boy who remembered long ago being anointed by Samuel the prophet. Had he not killed the lion and the bear? Slain Goliath? Had he not been helped by God again and again to find strength in weakness and victory in defeat? Had not God delivered him and his men when they were trapped on the rock? Had not the God of Israel smiled upon him and set the candle of the Lord upon his life? Would I be presumptuous to venture that perhaps the Spirit of God had revealed to David a glimpse of the messianic promise he carried in his loins? David was a prophet. All might have been lost around him, but David knew that God had not finished with him or with his little band of broken men. He knew that he carried the messianic dream and Seed in his loins.

On one hand, David's life, calling, and gifts were so high that few men or women have ever equaled his stature. And yet despite his high prophetic calling and the exalted heights from which he spoke, his life has remained accessible to men throughout the centuries. I believe the heart of David, as no other heart save our Lord's, has comforted more men and woman than any other figure in the narrative of human history. Where have the broken-hearted of Israel and the Church gone when they have sought comfort from the Lord? To David, the sweet psalmist of Israel, and his songs of deliverance in the night. David remembered for us in the dark what God had shown him in the light.

Perhaps God has given us David's life as an example? For in our small measure, we are all like David and can echo his plea:

> Hear my cry, O God;
> Give heed to my prayer.
> From the end of the earth I call to You when my heart is faint;
> Lead me to the rock that is higher than I. (Ps. 61:1-2)

The Story Did Not End There

The Lord did not merely console and strengthen David in his heart, but He also delivered him in time and space from his enemies, and what was taken from him and from his men was restored. After David had found new heart in God, he inquired of the Lord, asking Abiathar the priest, " 'Shall I pursue this band? Shall I overtake them?' And He said to him, 'Pursue, for you will surely overtake them, and you will surely rescue all' " (1 Sam.30:8).

David received a divine declaration of the restoration of all that he and his men had lost, and of total victory over his enemies. It is important to note here that David was not given all this promise for nothing, but with conditions. Salvation may be free, but receiving what is ours in His Kingdom always comes with a cost. What were the conditions put to David? "Rise up, pursue your enemy, and fight for what is yours." In other words, "If you can, once more by faith, rise up from the ashes and from your mourning and return to the breech of the battle. There, surely, you shall overtake them and recover all."

I believe that God will do great things for us, even miracles, and will pull victory out of the ashes of our defeated lives. He will give us life for death, if only we are willing to fight another day once more.

This is again Tolkien's "Eucatastrophe"—the good catastrophe—the sudden throwing down of what is wrong and setting up again of what is right. This is the heart of the universe and a wonderful secret. All will ultimately be set right. There is a happy ending to your story and to all stories. This is the Great Story of Christ and His Kingdom. This is the mystery of the resurrection and it is our story, too.

Only the Strong and the Weak Need Apply

David and six hundred of his men set out from Ziklag with the hope of recovering all, but on the way they came to the brook Besor, or in Hebrew, "the cold river." Jesus warned his disciples that the Kingdom of God would "suffer violent attacks," and only the violent would be able to "take it by force." We may take Jesus' words literally or metaphorically. Either way, throughout the ages, certain of God's servants have been called upon to resist violent attacks against the Kingdom of God, to rise up and put their own lives in jeopardy to rescue their brethren. They have been called upon to cross the brook Besor, the Cold River, in the service of their King and His Kingdom. However, not all of David's men had the strength to cross that cold river. Not all of us will have the strength to fight all of God's battles. Two hundred men stayed behind, too weak to pursue or fight.

David and four hundred men finally caught up with the Amalekites and utterly destroyed their army. Only a small band of young men managed to escape on camels. The Israelites recovered all—their wives, children, herds and possessions. Nothing was lost. They even managed to take a great spoil from the Amalekite camp. When they returned to the brook Besor, some of the baser men in David's company refused to share the spoil with those who had remained behind, but David resisted them. He gave them a command saying, "As his share is who goes down to the battle, so shall his share be who stays by the baggage; they shall share alike." The Scriptures tell us, "So it has been from that day forward, that he made it a statute and an ordinance for Israel to this day" (1 Sam. 30:24-25).

David's gesture expresses a great truth and insight into the heart of God and into the mystery of the true cost of the Kingdom. As we are all one Body: the Church and the Israel of God, we share alike in the spoils of the Kingdom's battles.

Yes, there are champions with great gifts and great strength. And there are the less gifted. But God's champions would be the first to tell us that their gifts and abilities are not for their benefit alone. I remember many years ago as a young Christian at Elim Bible Institute hearing Costa Deir refer to the gift ministries mentioned in the book of Ephesians. He read from Ephesians 4:11, "And He gave some as apostles, and some as prophets, and some as evangelists, and some as pastors and teachers." Then he said, "I am a gift to the Body of Christ." I was amazed and thought, that sounds a bit arrogant. But he continued, "Whatever ministry I or anyone has received from God is of grace and given, not to me or to you, but to the Body of Christ." In the final analysis, one can only give what one has received. Apparently God is satisfied if all we can give is our all—great or small. The strong know they are strong because God has made them strong. But who can know why the weak are weak? Perhaps they are weak because they were wounded and wearied in faithful service to their King long before they reached the brook Besor? God knows, and He is the one who ultimately distributes the spoils of His Kingdom.

The Mamertine Prison of Rome

The costs of the Kingdom are not equally shared. Some carry a heavier load than others, because God has enabled them to bear a heavier load. "To whom much is given, of him much will be required." David found strength in God and then shared his treasure with his men, their families, and finally with all the world and us. Many men and women of God have carried more than their share.

I can remember visiting the Mamertine prison in Rome. It was there that Paul was last imprisoned before his martyrdom. It is not a big prison. In fact, it is a small hole in the stony ground with two chambers and one distant source of natural light that barely illuminates the cells below. It is damp and dark and cold, and it was the last place the Apostle Paul rested his head before he was beheaded during the reign of Nero. I can see Paul shivering and writing his last testament to Timothy, "When you come, bring the cloak that I left at Troas with Carpus … Make every effort to come before winter" (2 Tim. 4:13-21).

There is something tragic, and yet beautiful in the end of Paul's natural life and ministry. After more than thirty years of sacrifice, persecutions, beatings, shipwrecks, and imprisonments for the sake of the gospel, Paul finds himself alone in a dark hole, abandoned by most of his co-laborers and by those he served in the ministry. From his last prison he writes to Timothy,

> You are aware of the fact that all who are in Asia turned away from me, among whom are Phygelius and Hermogenes ... Demas … has deserted me … Crescens … Titus … Alexander the coppersmith did me much harm … no one supported me, but all deserted me; may it not be counted against them. (2 Tim. 1:15; 4:10-16)

One wonders what any other man, someone like you or I, would have thought at the end of our life, shivering and alone in the Mamertine prison, abandoned by almost all our friends and even by most of our spiritual children. Rome was Paul's Ziklag. To any objective observer, Paul sat in the ashes of his life's work—rejected by the very Christians and churches he had served and to whom he had given his life. Did he despair? No. Paul was cut from the same Living Stone as David, and he could also say like David, "But the Lord stood with me and strengthened me, so that through me the proclamation might be fully accomplished, and that all the Gentiles might hear; and I was rescued out of the lion's mouth" (2 Tim. 4:17).

Out of his ashes he could say:

> For I am already being poured out as a drink offering, and the time of my departure has come. I have fought the good fight, I have finished the course, I have kept the faith; in the future there is laid up for me the crown of righteousness, which the Lord, the righteous Judge, will award to me on that day; and not only to me, but also to all who have loved His appearing. (2 Tim. 4:6-8)

Paul has his crown and we have his epistles to the churches and the example of his life—a life poured out to God for others.

This was and still is the cost of the Kingdom. Was it worth it? All that was lost? Ask the plumber. Ask the fishermen, the tax collector, the leper, the shepherd, the tentmaker. Ask C. T. Studd, Jim Elliot, ask yourself. Once the King has won our heart, we know that the cost of the Kingdom is less than nothing, just all that we are and have.

Ahmet the plumber was right: "Now, we have something much better than what we lost." And to this the Carpenter agrees.

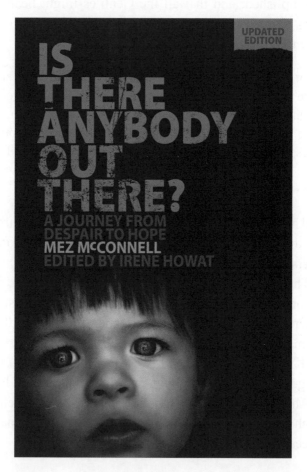

UPDATED
EDITION

IS
THERE
ANYBODY
OUT
THERE?

A JOURNEY FROM
DESPAIR TO HOPE
MEZ McCONNELL
EDITED BY IRENE HOWAT

ISBN 978-1-84550-773-2

Is There Anybody Out There?
A Journey from Despair to Hope
Second Edition

MEZ MCCONNELL

Since the publication of *A Child Called "It"* by Dave Pelzer, there hasn't been a story like this. But this is not just another harrowing story about an excruciating childhood and the ravages on a life it produces. The difference is that Mez not only escaped from his 'trial by parent' but he discovered a hope that has transformed his life. He in turn has helped others find hope in their lives. Mez's story is told with a frankness and wit that hides much of the pain and despair that was his everyday experience. Nevertheless, although his story at times may sicken you, his first brushes with the faith that restored him will make you laugh out loud! Mez's life involved abuse, violence, drugs, thieving and prison – but you don't have to fall as far as he in order to climb out of the traps in your life. Do you like happy endings? Mez still suffers from his experiences but you'll be amazed at how far you can be restored from such a beginning.

This is a compelling, gripping, heart-wrenching, you-can't-put-it-down story of sin and grace. Read this and thank God that, as Psalm 136 says, 'His love endures forever.'

Mark Dever
Senior Pastor of Capitol Hill Baptist Church, Washington, DC

Mez McConnell is now pastor for Niddrie Community Church, in Edinburgh, Scotland (partnered by Charlotte Chapel). Previously he was a missionary with Unevangelised Fields Mission (UFM) working with street kids in Brazil. He is married and has two children.

Christian Focus Publications

Our mission statement –

STAYING FAITHFUL
In dependence upon God we seek to impact the world through literature faithful to His infallible Word, the Bible. Our aim is to ensure that the Lord Jesus Christ is presented as the only hope to obtain forgiveness of sin, live a useful life and look forward to heaven with Him.

Our books are published in four imprints:

CHRISTIAN FOCUS

popular works including biographies, commentaries, basic doctrine and Christian living.

CHRISTIAN HERITAGE

books representing some of the best material from the rich heritage of the church.

MENTOR

books written at a level suitable for Bible College and seminary students, pastors, and other serious readers. The imprint includes commentaries, doctrinal studies, examination of current issues and church history.

CF4•K

children's books for quality Bible teaching and for all age groups: Sunday school curriculum, puzzle and activity books; personal and family devotional titles, biographies and inspirational stories – because you are never too young to know Jesus!

Christian Focus Publications Ltd,
Geanies House, Fearn, Ross-shire,
IV20 1TW, Scotland, United Kingdom.
www.christianfocus.com